Storm in a ‾

The best tea-shop
in Norwich!

Benjamin.

x

The Whisperings of Angels

The Correlation between our thoughts and beliefs and their effects on our lives

Benjamin Fairbairn

Contents

My Deepest gratitude to my positive partners and associates for their support and honesty and without whom this book would not be as it is today:
Aly Woods, Homivansh Foolessur and Ingrid Gegner.

To the many who went above and beyond to display inspirational examples of love, humanity and kindness:
Christian Haywood, Anne-Marie Cardorka, Cherri Mentessi, Magno Luis and Demi Smith.

And to my wonderful partner Olga, for her consistent belief, support, honesty and contribution.

Thank you to all I have not mentioned who also gave their great support and to contributors passed on. To the children born and yet to be born who give this world passion, reason and charm.

You are appreciated and loved.

Point-blank

Is the world I live in
So hard to figure out?
I feel my brain is losing touch
I don't know what it's about.

I feel my life is nothing.
I'm wasting it each day.
As I search to find myself
I feel I've lost my way.

I feel my life depleting
And age is creeping fast.
I'm trying to move forward
But I'm clinging to my past.

Things aren't happening for me at all
It seems it never will.
What is the use in trying
When I always come up nil?

Everything I was good at
I cannot say no more.
I've never put it to good use
Not knowing what it's for.

I'm trying hard to make a change
Whilst staying true to me.
I'm trying to keep my soul intact
But it doesn't want to be.
This is the hardest thing I've done.
Much too hard to say.
But I know my strength will get me through
I know I'll find my way.

I know I'll find myself again
For in my mind I trust.
And though I don't believe I can
I believe I must.

Nothing matters when the goal is to find
Peace inside my mind.
I'll dedicate myself to this
And leave the world behind.

Benjamin Fairbairn
1999

Part One

Why do we Suffer?

Our Intrinsic Link to a Dynamic Power

HOWEVER MUNDANE OR ROUTINE A life may seem, weaved in-between the fabric of each and every existence, young or old – rich or poor, lay intricate beauties, alive and buoyant - ripe for discovery. Magic and miracles are ceaselessly working at every single moment within us, within our entire planet and our extended universe. If we could only experience the vibrant colours of the activity that holds our existence together it would become abundantly clear that our possibilities are ever limitless. We are beautiful, magical and miraculous creatures imbibed with the consciousness to experience and respond to those experiences with choices stemmed from the impulsive to the deeply considered. We are possessed with the power to dream and to create using imagination through inspiration. We are gifted with the strength to transform existence and experience, to grow and to fortify and to inspire change from within and without. We've a unique opportunity over other lives on this planet to create and to enjoy creation. To bask in the beams of the sun's energy and to transform it into enjoyment and bliss. To nourish the soil and grow crops or to beautify a garden. We have an electric charge of opportunity flowing through the air, pulsing within the seas currents and propelling itself through the underground. One planet pulsing with such a dynamic power and we are living upon it.

How then do so many of us plod and trudge through our existence placing so little value on the very same magical and natural force that pulsates our life-blood through our bodies? How is it that the vast majority of us sit and dwell inside our own suffering, feeling the darkness of uncertainty slowly fill our lives like the flooding of a small cellar with a pungent and foul liquid? A mind that becomes the gates of confinement instead of the paths to freedom, squeezing us until life itself becomes transformed into an unfaceable and tragic burden that must be, through extreme depressions, hurt or destroyed in order for freedom to be achieved?

My first experience with self-harming came at the age of around nine. When we were sent to bed it was forbidden to come back down for any reason. When I was sent to bed, whilst laying in my bed in the darkness, I realised that I had somehow forgotten to say goodnight to my Ma. No big deal? To me this struck deep and an uncanny swell of anger came over me. Frustration caused my jaw to clamp and tears to flow. My body was filled to the surface with stinging emotion so I gripped at my stomach with clawed hands and tried to tear myself open and let it all out. Little damage was caused by the tiny hands but yet enough to cause a small bleeding that would leave scabs. Still to this day I don't know why I was so upset.

Isn't it fascinating the myths and illusions we build up in our heads and hearts that compel us to do no good to ourselves?

This may be a strange phenomenon but it is one that is neither new nor taboo. The rhetoric of the useless and pathetic life is wide-spread and ever-popular. It is viewed on our television screens and on the internet at every turn. The laborious life is preached and promoted in our music, movies, literature and on social media and it is being eagerly consumed by the masses as though it bore the taste of a moreish sweetness. Life sold as misery is big business... and business is thriving.

The evidence to the contrary, however, is all around us: close your eyes and think of a tree blowing in the breeze. The image is thrown upon something and it is seen with your inner-eye as real as if you were there right now in this moment. How is this possible? You can even hear the breeze and the rustling of the leaves. Think of a horse, running on a dirt road and all of the details are there. The soft auburn hair over the thick and muscular frame. The light falling upon every detail is perfect. The movement is as real as real can be. How is this so? We know our mind is there, however instead of basking in its miracles we suffer it.

Suffering brings with it a substance that is very quickly recognisable and relatable. Write a song of suffering and it is a smash-hit. Write a song considering the wonders of life and it quickly gets tossed upon the cheese-pile. We all seem to adore a bit of suffering. We bond over it, drink over it and use each-other's shoulders to cry over it.

These writings will attempt to place down the methods, strategies and attributes that I came to understand, through an experience that was - make no mistake - life-saving, as most necessary when designing an existence that is harmonious with the innate intentions and desires of the mind, body and soul and will point to aspects of my own story. This book is not intended as a gratification towards misery although it may sometimes seem that way. Instead it will document how I journeyed from a confining prison of suffering to the grand gardens of freedom. My own trajectory through suffering came from dying in one life to be reborn in the next, not through a physical death but through the death of certain limitations that I once lived by. The death of an old and the birth of a new. A transcendence from the lies of inertia to the truths of consistent movement. Lies that I told myself and wore as an armour, shielding me from a truth far more beneficial and brighter. It will *not* be a guide as which to live your life by, as every life is a story of its own and must unfold in its own manner, however if something you read is deemed as helpful I am pleased it can be useful to you.

This book is intended, not as a gospel to how things *should* be done, but instead as a *possibility* of the way that things *could* be done and to the un-deniability that it can be achieved pari passu to the ebbs and flows of our lives.

What this is, is what proved useful for me and what I see all around me as a result of the directions I decided to walk in my own existence. It is also my observation via the perspective I hold at the time of writing. It is the results of the dissections of my experiences and sufferings and how I actively sought to find another way forward in peace.

Here I will attempt to translate the methods I learned through experience, observation and personal study. From as early as the age of fourteen I began to take note in the form of diaries, which indicated a need to understand what was happening to me in my life. I formulated theories regarding the suffering and confusion that I was experiencing and desperately tried to design methods and techniques for dealing with them. It was only much later in life that I began to study books, seminars, recordings and essays to either confirm, correct or modify my observational and experiential theories. The essays ranged from a sociological, scientific, meta-physical and theological points of view and also from the perspectives of tactical war and martial-arts experts. As well as this I gained insight from the people I would interview informally; friends and strangers alike, with interesting theories and experiences in life. Through all of this, I gathered information with the attempt to form a concise understanding of a life with very interesting results.

Many of the methods may be controversial and may even seem arrogant at first. They may go against much of what you may have lived your life by up to this point, yet it is my great hope that you persevere and read with an open mind and enjoy the experience that imbued me with a freedom that I had never known as a young and hopeless darkling. I will also state that, within these writings I make no attempts to promote any religious belief whatsoever. I admire and find inspiration in a plethora of different beliefs and may quote such from here and there. As previously explained, take from this what you will, I ask only that you read with a mind boundless from presumption as to fully enjoy.

Abuse Confusion

I ONCE ASKED MYSELF A VERY interesting question: "Was he truly abusive?"

That question came one month and one week after my father had passed away. My father was a clever man. He was caring and kind and *so* charismatic. When you saw him with his Grand-children and heard him speak regarding his family, his actions were that of a deep love and his words were that of pure commitment to their hearts and their well-being. Perfect as he would seem, my father was also a man of severe cruelty. His mannerisms and movements, words and sounds seemed designed to intimidate. His rhetoric would be that he gave us life and could take it away at any point if needs be. How could these two apparently different men exist within the same body? And what effect does this have on the young minds of those that are exposed to the two?

Is this just an over-stated judgement of an over-sensitive man who has always been looking for a dramatic relationship with his Father? Possibly. Could the incidents that occurred be few and far between yet has remained at the forefront of my memories? Possibly. If that is the case, then was he actually abusive at all? After all isn't parenthood a learning curve for all parents? Do all parents get it right all the time? Do all children have memories of their parent's that were not so pleasant? Does this make their parents abusers also? While I was working in a school, there was a situation with a boy who turned up with his hat on and, when instructed by a teacher to remove the hat, the boy steadily refused. When asked once again by the teacher to remove his hat the child said that he didn't want to and asked to speak to the teacher privately to explain why. It turned out that the boy had been behaving badly at school and his sister's boyfriend, as a punishment, shaved his hair aggressively and sent him to school. The boy's hair had been shaved right down the middle and a large chunk taken out of the side. Was this abuse? The boy had misbehaved and the family had probably heard enough after being sent continuous letters and phone calls. Maybe they felt powerless to change the boy's wicked ways. Perhaps the man had felt the need to do something radical to change the way the boy behaved and thought that this would really shake him up enough to put him back on the correct path? Obviously this was an over-reaction but was it really abuse?

I think that to answer the question honestly we could refer to a few different things in the aspect of the role of the adult to the child. Not the perceived role but the actual role. A child, until it is an adult, is an automatic vulnerable person in that they cannot adequately feed themselves, house themselves or protect themselves. When the child becomes an adult they will need to know how to do these things in order to survive and maintain themselves at the very least or to prosper and excel at the very highest expectation. These things do not just appear at the age of eighteen. They have to be nurtured and taught and this is done by the people who are around them. But the people around them will only teach them what they have learned themselves. Everything we say and do to a child is learned by them even if they are unaware of the learning and we, unaware of the teaching. They learn and take it through life with them.

So what did the boy, with the sporadically shaved head learn? What would you have learned? I know I would feel powerless and intimidated by the act of having my head shaved by an angry man much bigger than I was. I would feel fear of ridicule, fear of being beaten up. Just massive fear. And of my respected peers? I would feel the fear of that respect disappearing and I'd hope I don't run into that girl that I liked. I would feel like skulking off into a dark corner to hide. I would wish to become invisible or that the world would open up and swallow me whole just not to be seen by anyone. Or even worse, I could wish I was dead. I had done something so terrible that it merited the world turning against me. I have learned fear and how to be fearful and if I ever have a son, god-forbid that he remind me of this day by misbehaving for if he does I would punish him so hard he would never forget it!

If, through your actions, the only thing you teach a child is fear, anxiety, self-hate and anger, then you *have* abused the child, you have abused your position as a teacher and you have abused the future. The seed of suffering has been planted by you and it will grow inside this helpless child until it becomes the adult. Then it will pass on its learnings to the new generation and so forth until a new seed is planted. *If* a new seed is ever planted at all.

My father may have been caring, kind and charismatic sometimes but he was also abusive. The qualities of caring kindness, love and protection combined with the harmful existence of abuse only creates the seed of confusion.

But what do I mean by abuse? Surely abuse is just a matter of perspective? If the parent's actions created the seed of fear in the child then maybe that child was just really fearful in the first place. Perhaps it simply had fertile soil for fearful seeds? So where did this fearful nature come from? Always a seed and always planted by our first teachers. There are no exceptions.

Children are not fearful by nature.

For me in particular, the experiences that I remember as a child contained very confusing and harmful behaviour. One such experience was as follows:

One beautiful Sunday, my Mother and my sisters had gone to church and I had stayed in bed. I didn't want to go to church as I found it very boring. I didn't tell my Mother that but I just didn't wake up, purposefully in order not to go. My Father had asked me then to go to the local shop to buy his newspaper. This would have been the first time I'd been allowed to go out of their sight, on my own, in my life so far. He gave me the money and told me to wait for the change after buying the paper and then to walk back the same way I'd came. He also told me to cross the road in front of the house so he could check that I was doing it safely. As I walked out, crossed the road and made my way down the street I was filled with so many different thoughts. I remember the air being crisp and cool and the trees rustling with a very gentle breeze. The sun was beaming. This was *my* day. I kept putting my arms out either side of me just to confirm to myself that I was walking to the shop on my own. I felt so great and confident and really felt that this was a real step to me growing up as a person. *My Dad had allowed me to go out and get his paper.* I remember the feeling in my chest. Big. Full. Proud. Walking back, I had a flick through to the cartoons. Caught a gist of what it was about so I could look forward to reading it later on and then I was at the house on the opposite side of the road. Time to cross. So I looked left and right and crossed the road. When I got through the door my father grabbed me by the shoulder, without looking at me and led me to the living-room where he removed the news-paper from me and threw it to the table before slapping me across the jaw and onto the chair. He grabbed me back up by my upper-arm with his right hand and the lower part of my face with his left and squeezed hard. He brought his face very close to me and his teeth were clenched. He spoke something to me and I blubbered back "yes daddy. Sorry daddy." Then he threw me to the side and told me to get out of his sight. As I left he called me a "little arse-hole". I went to my room in absolute confusion as I had no idea what I had done wrong. I knew I got the right paper and he didn't even ask me for the change. What could I have done? My head was throbbing and I couldn't think straight. I now felt angry that the world was sunny and the air was crisp outside. I felt angry when I heard the children playing outside. I was feeling miserable so why was the sun still shining? My curtains were drawn and the room was dark but a crack of light still taunted me. It turned out that he had seen me flicking through his papers on the way back as he was looking through the window. I heard him telling my mum when she arrived back with my sisters. I hated them when they got back. Why were they allowed downstairs and I wasn't? My dad was a wonderful cook and had made fried rice with sausages for lunch. I knew because I could smell it and I knew the sound of it cooking. I heard my Mother ask if I should be called down to eat and, although I didn't hear the response, I can only assume that the answer was no. Now I felt *hatred* for all of them for eating without me. I could smell the food, hear the T.V and the cutlery clanging against the plates and my seed of hate was being watered. Shortly after, one of my sisters, had quietly peeked into my room. She whispered to ask if I was alright and I nodded yes even though my bottom lip and chin ached with the real answer. She smiled and wiggled her fingers bye and closed the door behind her. Now I hated myself for hating her.

On this day I learned confusion, pain, hatred, fear and to not read the paper on the way home. At least to not get caught.

In the book: Bushido-The Way of the Samurai, based on the Hagakure by Tsunetomo Yamamoto, there is a very interesting excerpt regarding the raising of children and the responsibility of, not only the parent, but all those who cross the child's path:

"First, inspire them with courage, even when they are very small. You must never scare them nor deceive them, even in a joke. If they contract cowardice while young, the cowardice will last the whole life. Hence cowardice will become their life-long fault."

The Samurai had very specific goals when raising their children and, although I believe the Hagakure to be mostly outdated, it does inspire some good ideas when it comes to general parenting. Another quote states that: *"you must direct them so that they learn by themselves"* which allures to guidance rather than commands. Principles as the foundation for rules. In his study 'Childhood and Adolescence', John Arthur Hadfield stated regarding the raising of children "...while we cannot lay down rules, because so much depends on the circumstances of the case, we can be guided by *principles*. Rules are concerned mainly with behaviour, whereas principles depends on *aims* or *ends* in raising the child. If we were guided on principles, we ask ourselves why we do these things, what will be the result of this or that treatment, and vary our treatment in accordance to those ends."

So does this mean that my Father's loving and caring nature was unreal? That the good memories I have are non-valid because of the actual abuse received? I don't believe so. As people we are much more complicated than just one thing or the other. All of our thoughts come from our experiences and our experiences from our thoughts. We build expectations based on our experiences and perpetuate those experiences because we expect them to happen. We do what we have learned to do and we have learned the lessons of our childhood with very little choice in the matter. This, of course, includes our parents. We grow in what we know, with whatever seed that has been planted, and we all come to own our thoughts, our own choices, our own decisions and our own destinies. What we have learned in our past does not have to be repeated by us in the future and yet without conscious intervention it very well may. We can choose to break the cycle by facing our past sufferings and watching it leave us. It is not easy, indeed it is the hardest thing in life to do. However, if we do not, it will continue to follow us and our children no matter where we choose to hide. This way we can be free to raise our children, not by a schematic forged by our parents and theirs before them, but in a way that we see beneficial to their growth as individual beings for the good of all those and the world around them. Our responsibilities remain vast.

As we've spoken about abusive behaviour and the confusion this can bring, as well as our own responsibilities to the beings in this life, we can now begin to take a good look at how our past has affected the way we may treat and have treated those around us. As challenging as it is to analyse the behaviour that befalls us, it takes a real strong sense of awareness to be able to look deeply at our very own. To stand naked and vulnerable in front of ourselves and say "this is what I have done and this is why I think have done it".

When we have been treated unfairly or abusively the last thing on our mind is forgiveness and sometimes this lack of being able to forgive, as time goes on, can make a morbid transition into resentment. Why should we forgive? Why should *we* take responsibility for the actions of someone that has hurt us?

There is also the very damaging misconception and popular belief that forgiveness only comes *after* the one who hurt us has apologised.

As a twenty-three year-old boy, I had an affinity towards the macabre. I loved horror and monsters. I still do enjoy a good horror movie (although good horror movies can be hard to find by today's standards). My bedroom at my parent's house, where I still lived, had black walls, the curtains were always pulled shut and horror memorabilia adorned every wall and shelf. I had an eighteen inch toy figurine of Ash, the main character from the Evil Dead movies, complete with boom-stick (sawn-off shotgun) and chainsaw hand. It had a motion sensor that would make it speak anytime anything passed by it and my three year-old nephew found this absolutely terrifying.

My sister's children are very dear to me and I have always felt very close to them and when two of my sister's first children were born in 2001, I immediately felt an immense responsibility toward them. Not to mention a huge amount of expectations for them.

By this time in my life, due to my past experiences, I had already affirmed that "I would never beat on anyone unless they had the power to beat on me right back" and this included my nephews. I really wanted to do my part to raise them in a different way to the way that I'd been raised; it was normal for us to get "smacks" and full beat-downs were commonly expected. But I had to be different. I really wanted to show everyone that the old kind of brutality didn't have to continue.

One afternoon, as I was sitting on the sofa, I had called my nephew over to me and for one reason or another he had given me a slap clean across my face. Three year-olds don't need much of a reason to slap anything but the emotions that flooded me were deep. My mind immediately became extremely busy with the right way to handle this in a way that would be different to everybody else. I wouldn't beat him. I wouldn't even shout at him but I had to somehow let him know that he couldn't just go around slapping people. So I had an idea. I decided to pick him up and take him to my dark, black room, adorned with beasts and monsters and the giant Ash figure that spoke when activated, and I decided to leave him in there. I dropped him in the middle of the room and walked over to the door. He was begging me in the only way he knew how, by crying and saying over and over again "no no no I don't want to!" and I looked at him and said; "Stay there and don't move until I come to get you. If you move Ash will get you. You don't slap! Now stay there and don't move." Then I left him sitting in the dark room surrounded by monsters. Crying and afraid in the dark. I left him there for half of an hour... When I went back to get him, I hugged him and told him that he must never slap and that it was naughty. His tears had dried onto his face. He was afraid and sorry and never wanted that to happen to him anymore. He never slapped me again.

So my method had worked, right? My nephew didn't slap me ever again so everything was good... Right? I hadn't beaten him or hit him or even threatened to hit him and he was never in any real danger. Nothing was going to physically harm him and I knew I would let him out and hug him later so this was all okay... Right? Is this all sounding familiar?

Loving kindness mixed with cruelty, for all my good intentions, was the way I had chosen to teach my young nephew and I was very proud of the way I had handled this situation. I didn't beat him and I didn't shout at him therefore felt I had broken the cycle. For all my good intentions I had decided that I would teach the child by using his vulnerability and fear. I would scare him. I abandoned what I believed was cruel, in the physical instilling of fear through beatings, and adopted a new approach that I believed was a lot more humane, the mental instilling of fear through abandonment and just plain petrification. I repeat the quote from the Hagakure: *"First, inspire them with courage, even when they are very small. You must never scare them nor deceive them, even in a joke. If they contract cowardice while young, the cowardice will last the whole life. Hence cowardice will become their life-long fault."*

My three year-old nephew learned fear that day and that is my responsibility and I suffered it for a long time. How then do we relinquish ourselves from our suffering and can we ever break free from the cycle that we have found ourselves spinning through?

Note: Since writing this I have spoken to and apologised to my nephew (now eighteen). He has told me that he doesn't remember a thing.

Benjamin Fairbairn

The Darkling

THROUGH THE MULTIPLE PAINFUL AND confusing occurrences experienced, I began to fortify hate within my bones. Hate was clear and as it eased the pain I was feeling as the darkling was being formed. During my past years as a darkling I suffered everything that fell before my senses and what I foresaw within my future days was nothing than so much more suffering. My countenance was happy yet internally, grave misery and disparity was rapidly unfolding. Unknowingly I developed abilities that allowed me to experience and understand suffering as intimately as I could. This strange form of suffering that crosses the border of some kind of enjoyment and comfort, which became a sort of therapy to me and allowed me insights and momentary escapes from a world I didn't want to be a part of. Unfortunately this also gave me the idea that my misery was my gift as it allowed me to create things that I believed made me somebody and without it I may become an unrecognisable nobody. I sought after my suffering and it eventually became precious to me like my own child. Even to this day, I can look back fondly upon some of my more dramatic sufferings however, what I was actually experiencing became a mental and emotional agony that I did not understand how or why it was occurring and had no idea of the catalyst. I wished to be recognised as a powerful and unstoppable juggernaut at times and other times I found myself embodying the reclusive Grendel. Crouched in a darkened corner, embracing my knees, rocking back and forth and comforting my suffering. My home. My refuge. My very own child.

Violence became a natural outlet for the suffering. The thought of strong bone crushing and pounding into weaker bone released a tension for me at the time and the more violent I became, the more violent the world I lived in seemed to be. I know now that I was experiencing a fear of life. I feared the good in my life turning to suffering so I tried to head it off and transform it to suffering but on my own terms. Suffering that I could somehow use to become stronger. I studied the grim. Serial killers and victims of severe, physical trauma were two of my favourite musings. I would stare at wide open faces and mangled bodies in my spare time and reimagined them as living, loving beings that were now nothing but clumps and lumps of so much meat, bone and sinew – what was alive was now dead and nothing more. All that life, now nothing but meat. I felt that if I could somehow nullify everything that may shock or strike fear into me or anything that may cause me some emotional trauma down the line, if I could somehow become numb to this, then surely this would make me fearless and nothing then would be able to hurt or expose me, leaving me vulnerable and weak. The idea was to head-off my fears before they got to me. The problem arose when I discovered that the more I fed my fear, the more fearful I became.

I found that I feared death. Not so much my own but the death of my family and of my loved ones. My friends. To lose them was an unthinkable circumstance to me. I would watch them speaking in conversation and I'd pretend that I was experiencing a flashback of when they were once alive - long after they had died - and I would die a little inside. My imagination, vivid, grim and unstoppable, would picture my family as the images I frequented. I feared my minds activity and I grew to hate myself because of this.

I discovered that I feared rejection. In my mind I wasn't really a person at all. Women didn't find me alluring and men found me a non-threatening weakling, little more than ether and little less than substance. But it was all in my mind so sometimes these thoughts would go away. If I would one day take the risk and ask the girl on a date or join the conversation with the others and should experience rejection, all my fears would then inescapably be confirmed, rising from a fear of reality to actualising within reality itself and I would have nowhere to hide from this exposure. So I kept away from the risks. Away from the danger of exposure and failure.

Although I had no fear of dying, as I placed little value upon my own life, I feared being forgotten once dead. I would imagine myself as a ghost spectating at my own funeral, floating above and around watching everybody closely for their responses to my passing. My mother seemed to be crying but no-one else. They looked sad, but not torn apart like I would like them to be. Perhaps they were bored? Children ran and played as my casket lowered. As time went on day-by-day I would observe them, as the spectre, floating watching over them in the front-room, the kitchen, at their work-places, going about their daily lives. They would laugh and eat and play with children and watch the TV. It seemed that I was forgotten and now I was dead *and* I was gone. I had left them nothing to remember me by and that would not do. I yearned to be remembered forever. I had realised my mortality and saw everything as death. I became angry that we had to die and that I would eventually, regardless of what I had achieved or how many things I had seen, be completely forgotten. From a life to a death to a memory to a nothingness. So I went about to become over-exuberant in a way that, whilst keeping my walls up, kept the delusion as strong as was needed and I became the clown. The outrageous and vicious buffoon. Being the fool surely meant that everyone would miss me when I was gone. There was no other legacy I knew how to forge. As long as I was missed, for whatever reason, that was all that concerned me.

Benjamin Fairbairn

The Porcupine

REGARDLESS OF WHAT I DID for a living, at this point my profession was that of a full time porcupine. I was constantly surrounding myself and hiding within a spikey exterior and my greatest goal was to run away to avoid any impending pain. I wanted to run and, without questioning this goal, it seemed like the perfect plan to do so. Run from the pain in the past. Run from the projected pain in the future and run also from the pain that was riddling my present.

I figured that, if I ran fast enough, then I wouldn't be able to see what it was that I was afraid of. Of course, my logic at the time suggested that, if I couldn't see what I was afraid of then it would have no effect on me. But on one Saturday night, whilst out on a date, crying until the tears burned my face and eyes, everything changed. I can remember vividly, sitting in the streets, perched on a step with my head in my hands, blubbering uncontrollably like a starving baby. Sobbing whilst saliva and mucus attacked my visage and my words, held captive by a struggling lung, were morphed by wails of woe and confusion. Nothing attractive whatsoever. Needless to say this didn't go down well with the lady by my side at the time. I remember being overwhelmed to the point where I just didn't have the power to stop the tears from flowing. They poured out. I cracked and I fell and I was helpless. The next morning brought reflection. I thought back and noticed that the night before offered no spikey exterior to protect me. I

hadn't dropped it nor had I forgotten to put it on. It had just abandoned me...
It simply wasn't there.

What do you do when something that you had spent your whole life
forging to protect you disappears when you need it most? To find excuses for
you? To bestow unto you your aggression and your bravado? I decided then
that I had to stop running.

And what was the impending pain that I was running from? What was it
that I was so afraid of that I could not even face my own life? I used to think
that it was something specific but I soon found out that I was simply afraid
of everything. It didn't look that way of course. That's what a spikey exterior
does. More so then protects, it is a deterrent from anything getting too close.

My plan was always to run. In the past I had run away from home three
times and I ran because I felt my life depended on it and it most probably
did. One time in particular was when I was applying for a job as a Marvel
comics illustrator which came to an abrupt and unexpected end. This job
would have seen me travelling sporadically to New York and I was damn
excited about the whole thing. This was my chance to escape into the world.
My father had been recently made redundant and had been drinking one
evening and, somehow, he conjured the idea that I had made a joke about his
lack of employment, which wasn't true of course. Nevertheless he asked to
speak to me outside. Perhaps it was no surprise to me that he wanted to
speak to me with his fists. As much as I tried to reason a way out of it, I knew
him well and knew that this would not work. I turned and I ran and this time,
I ran into homelessness which lasted for just over a year, sleeping in the
park, the odd church and squats with other homeless people. I escaped into
the world for sure, but not quite how I anticipated. How I rose from
homelessness will be addressed in a further medium.

The third time was when I stayed out of the home for good. This all
devastated me in some way as I really did want a close relationship with my
father, yet he seemed to not want to reciprocate.

Much later in our relationship my father, obviously when no one else was around, issued me with an apology; "Son", he said to me "I know I have treated you rough sometimes. Sometimes you have taken the brunt of my temper. That's because I'm going through a lot; up here...", tapping his head, "... and you're the only one who can take it. Your mother can't take it and your sisters can't take it. You're strong. You're my son and I do it to you because I know that you can take it." ... At least I think that was supposed to be an apology. All of this left me quite confused as he was my example. I may understand that my father may have suffered and that his suffering as a child was not fair. I can understand that. I do not, however, respect or condone his method of therapy in the brutalising of his family and the punishment dealt to me because he felt that I could "take it". We have all, at one time or another, experienced suffering in our lives and it is up to us how we process it. I would suggest that the best way is not to lock it away and punish others with your pain. All of this confused the hell out of me. I was in a completely confused state of mind. This confusion continued for as long as I felt that I "needed" answers from my father. What I actually needed was to be released from the grip of responsibility to find answers for his actions so I could be free to determine actions of my own that could be useful to my existence.

Back to the point of the porcupine and the falling of the spines. The protection I spent years of emotional effort creating had faded when I least expected it to and had left me vulnerable and on my knees in public, but how and why did this occur? Referring once more to the story of Beowulf, the hero is assigned with the mission to destroy the demon that is terrorising the local village, a mission which he boldly accepts, but when he arrives to face the demon, it instead strikes a deal with him. If he would lock it away and let it live, it would bestow upon him a life of dreams and riches equal to none. He would be strong and respected and he would live a life of power and happiness to a ripe and prestigious age. Beowulf agreed to the deal and locked the demon away within the cave. Upon his arrival at the village he spoke of how he had defeated and killed the demon in battle and Beowulf went on to live a life of fortune and prosperity as king. Yet years down the line and when it was least expected, the demon returned, destroying all that Beowulf had come to love including Beowulf himself. But first it utterly destroyed his entire world. Instead of slaying the demon, Beowulf locked it away and expected it to stay buried within the darkness. I had done the same thing and I had done it through ignorance of another possibility. I had built into an idol the image of my father. He was my hero and, piece by piece he eroded his own legend with deeply upsetting behaviour. Strangely enough it wasn't his treatment of me that I found detrimental but the contradictions to his own character and ideals that I had built around him. What had dissolved my resolve was the illusion that, regardless of what I did or what I believed, regardless of the work that I put into my conviction nor how hard I would try, the sins of the father would be repeated by me in my own future. I had discovered that my father was not only imperfect but that he had the capacity to be cruel and callous and violent and harmful and untrustworthy to those he was supposed to love and protect and educate. I feared myself becoming the same. I felt that I had been hardwired to become what I feared and I had no idea what to do about that. So one beautiful night, while out on a date, when everything was in place for a wonderful evening, everything all of a sudden fell and shattered to pieces.

I love language. Words are a marvellous way to communicate yet I find it challenging when it comes to describing exactly why I broke. My protection had left me. My armour had been compromised. It had simply taken too much damage over time and had broken away.

Earlier in the book I mentioned the lies that I told myself that were limiting my progression into a happier and more fulfilled life. Those lies were in the idea that this world was a pointless one and that I was insignificant. That people don't really have the capacity to love, to care, to cure. That everybody was just a psychopath in disguise. Of course we all have dualism when it comes to our characters – it is this complexity that makes us human, yet we also have the capacity for uncanny kindness and beauty. Yet believing this at the time felt like it would not have helped me in any way, to survive within the environment in which I grew. There was no space for that, so I cast aside thoughts of a beautiful world and with it, I believe, a healthy part of my sanity.

My life from this point became a lazy indulgence into meaninglessness. I had no time for good souls. I fought and I drank and fought. The more gristle I could find the better. The more blood and bone and meat. I had a fascination with us being nothing but sentient meat. Accidently conscious but nothing more than meat walking around and pretending to have a purpose and we were all just waiting to be dead.

I escaped this mental anguish, this prison, by realising, first, that I was actually even in one. I felt the walls and the confinement and the claustrophobia and I saw others who were free. The key to the confines of the prison was realising that there were no prison guards. There was no security and there was no set sentence. I had discovered the judge, the jury and the executioner, and I had found them all to be me. I had imprisoned myself. It is true that I was poorly treated, beaten and abused by one who I had loved and trusted and it seemed evident that emotional resilience was not an agenda that was important in my upbringing, but I hadn't been locked away by anyone. I had been *given* the key that I used to lock myself away. Just as a nurturing parent offers the key to confidence to their child, another parent can hand over the key to imprisonment. Yet it is always the child who uses the key to lock themselves away. This is no reason to now blame and strike yourself down in a flurry of self-pity as this all happens unconsciously. I had no idea what I was doing to myself and when I realised that I was the key, I began look deeply at the person who I had become. At who I was and I realised that I was somebody who had been passed the baton to administer suffering upon the child within. I realised that the anger, the hatred, the pain and the hopelessness was a reflection of what I was feeling inside. I had found the key and the hard work followed of finding my way out of the prison and its labyrinthian hallways. Which was not an easy exit to find. For years onwards I would sit within the hallways, with no clue as to how to escape.

So many search for an answer without ever thinking about what the question actually is. I did so much evaluating, in fact that's all that I ever did. I would evaluate and then I would suffer upon my evaluations. This only served to bring me to the summit of my mental sufferings as I still believed that my experience was pre-determined by everybody else's actions and not my own. My life was everybody's fault. A purely extrinsic consequence. This was all occurring within my own perception and, although everything from the outside seemed calm, turbulence wreaked havoc from within.

Be this as it may, the abilities that I conjured during these times, as previously mentioned, was the writing of journals and poetry, drawings and sculpture. This allowed me to pour out with great regularity; my great confusion and rage. And what would my days have been like without this outlet? I can assure you that, with no methods of expressing the something that was consistently tearing bits and pieces out of me, I may not have been here to write this today. Without the ability to somehow release the pressure that was building within me, there was no end to the destruction that could have been caused, the line of which, can only be drawn by your own imagination.

Suicide

IN MY TEENAGE YEARS, ONE thing I purposely veered from contemplating, regardless of how terrible I felt, was to end my life by suicide as I had decided long before that suicide was for the "weak ones" and, although I did want my life to end, I had made a promise to myself to not be the one who would end it. I had decided that I would take everything that life threw at me and I would shake my fist in defiance whenever life would try to dis-mantle me: *"Here you filthy and pointless life!"* I would say to myself at night whilst laying on my back, staring up into the vast blackness, *"Throw as you will for you cannot break me! I will never crumble and crawl to you. I am defiant! You will throw until you become a tired life and will bore of trying to break me because I will never give in!"* Gallant as this may have seemed, it was ultimately as foolish as it was futile. I *am* happy that I had such defiance or I may have ended my life swiftly as I saw little point to it. But while my defiance was strong it was poorly aimed and while I was shaking my fist at life, life was patiently taking my orders and serving me whatever I bleated, wherever I bleated it and however often my bleats were received. What I was suffering from was not life. I was only ever suffering from my own thoughts.

I had a particular view of the world that augmented life into something that was noxious and unfair. A filter that sifted out the good before it reached my perception. Life was always unbiased in its serving and continued to be so, serving me exactly as I demanded of it and the more I saw the more I demanded and the more I demanded the more I suffered. The cycle of suffering continued long enough to forge habits that perpetuated my suffering which grew more potent with time. Spinning out of control within this cyclone of rage I was finally and powerfully flung loose only to land in a thousand broken pieces before a magnanimous energy I had never known before. Slowly and painstakingly I pieced myself back together, this time looking to each piece before replacing, and cleansing it of as much anger, resentment and any other such filth and grit as I possibly could.

We can most surely go so far in healing ourselves, yet without the love, compassion and kindness from others and without professional intervention, we will always go so far and no further. Speaking to professionals can be an extremely difficult thing to come to terms with due to the stigma that is tied onto our shrinks and quacks. Yet these people have studied character and behaviour patterns in great depth and may hold the ability to offer some truly beneficial advice, information and guidance. It is true that we would much rather talk to our bestie when we're suffering through our traumas and it does come with the added bonus of having a beer at the same time. However with professional aid, you need not intoxicate in order to justify spilling your heart out. Their profession is to listen deeply and offer a viewpoint that guides you to revelation. It may be scoffed at yet I would advise to save your beer tokens and take a step toward somebody who can actually help you onto a transformative path. You'll be glad you did.

I no longer believe that suicide is a question of whether one is weak or strong but a question of what it is that one believes of the nature of life. If, which is quite common, one would believe that we are nothing but accidental, insignificant and self-important germs inhabiting a floating rock that is destined to implode into itself someday and all and every deed is pointless because of so, then when life becomes bombarded with suffering and there *seems* to be no *perceived* way out, then suicide is not such a far cry. It is an inconsequential end to a pointless suffering.

Some may even believe that to continue on in such cases would be the weak thing to do and that to end a life at this point would be considered as a merit for a badge of bravery. But, again, it is less about bravery but perception. What one *believes* is the prime reason for the outcomes experienced in their lives.

In the movie *"Sliding Doors"* the viewer is given the opportunity to see the life of a certain woman from two sides of the same spectrum beginning with her standing on a train platform and initiating the question: what if she was to miss her train? And also, what if she were to *catch* her train? We then witness the thread of the same life unravel from two separate possibilities and their outcomes thereon. Whatever you may think of the movie, wouldn't it be wonderful if we could do the same with our own lives? To see all of the possible outcomes before they occurred so we could make the perfect choice? I don't think so. Where would be the fun in that? It is true that we can predict and work towards that prediction, not stopping until it becomes true, as is the story with the rain-dancer who, every time he would dance it would eventually rain. The locals, stunned by his miraculous abilities asked him one day how he was able to cause the sky to fall with rain every time he danced. He answered "It's simple. I just keep dancing until it rains". We too can harness the ability to not stop until we get what we want yet, on this course, things will simply occur that we will not be prepared for. When this occurs it will be the perceptions, beliefs and habits that we have developed that will determine whether they are "fair" or not. Some will shake their fist and scream at god and others will fall to their knees in pain and woe. Others still will see the opportunity to learn and grow and become imbued with an altogether new power and a new path.

I have chosen to believe that life and its ways are, by its nature, incredibly challenging regardless of anything or whatever we may do, however much money we make, whether we get the girl of our dreams or how genetically gifted we may be. Life is just challenging most of the time and it is the choices that we make in light of the challenges that determine the level of happiness or suffering that we experience.

Benjamin Fairbairn

Abundance, Gratitude and the route to Compassion

Lack attack and the mystery of abundance

CONSIDERING THE STATE OF LACK that we sometimes find ourselves in, it can be infuriating when somebody decides to tell us that all beings on this planet have been gifted with complete and limitless abundance. That the natural law of supply states that we need not mine for breathable air and that our planet's surface is three quarters water. That water also exists in the air, in the ground as moisture and in the ice-caps. That we also have a high percentage of water in our bodies at all times. It may not mean much to those who feel in a state of lack that water is our greatest means of sustenance and it is absolutely everywhere and available to most of us with the turning of a tap. That our food grows from the ground, on the trees and bushes and moves through the land, sea and air continuously. That we have a natural cycle that brings the sun up to a tolerable temperature, regardless of how hot or cold it may become, and a moon that controls the tides with its tractive force of clockwork precision and yet we still may complain about the weather. If our planet moved a fraction off of its axis away from the sun we'd all freeze to death. If it moved a fraction off of its axis towards the sun the entire planet would burn to a cinder. It would seem, as far as nature is concerned, that we are quite blessed. It may be infuriating to hear all this when in a state of lack yet that does not alter the truth that we are basking in abundance. Lack is a personal choice and is due to a refusal to accept the actuality of abundance. Let me be clear, having no money is far from lack.

Having no money just means that you have not yet become aware of how to use the abundant resources available in order to attain money or that you are in a state of creating that awareness. True lack is a lack of the knowledge of how to remove yourself from suffering.

We are living in abundance right now.

"From abundance he took, and still abundance remained"

The Upanishads

Of course there are natural circumstances that brings, let's say; the weather to extreme conditions that can cause death and dismay to many living things, yet these disasters only appear so from our own perceptions not from the perceptions of the natural cycle of things as this planet is doing what it has always done: move, augment and survive. Sometimes it freezes and sometimes it swelters. Sometimes it floods and other times it droughts. These are all natural cycles of the planet; the perception of "good" and "bad" is our own. This world is teeming over with an abundance of miraculous and magical activity that benefits all of us within every single moment yet it happens with such an amazing perfection that we hardly ever take the time to notice and to be grateful. We fully recognise, however, when something goes wrong.

I'm not suggesting that we should maintain gratitude if we lose everything in a "natural disaster". That's ridiculous. I'm saying that the tragedy is the loss of everything and not the planet's natural motion. That would be the blame we attach to the loss.

Case in point: Our hearts (the magical muscular organ that begins its arduous work the moment it is formed in the womb and continues to do so until we leave this life... and sometimes, in some cases, for longer) pump approximately seven litres of life-blood through itself in every single minute. Seven-thousand-six-hundred within each day and two-hundred-million litres within one complete life-time yet we only ever seem to pay it attention when it palpitates and stops. Our bodies have constructed within itself many filtration systems so that the air, gifted to us by our planet's atmosphere, when inhaled by us, is fed into the mighty lung which filters the oxygen from the carbon-dioxide, which is then fed back into the air through the nose and mouth leaving the oxygen which is gifted to our blood-stream. The heart says "thank you lung." Lung responds with: "no, thank you heart!" They work in unison and are gracious to each other. It is not just a simple, arbitrary occurrence, it is a deliberate transaction between all life on this world and the worlds beyond. Yet we only ever pay it notice when it hurts, when we struggle for breath or when we witness the death rattle pass the lips of a loved one.

However, all these miracles will continue to occur within us whether we choose to focus upon it or not. When we settle down for the night our bodies continue its life-long purpose despite our choices. Working and working and working still. Your body, whether you were born short, tall or with no ears, is altogether a perfect creative mechanism within itself and it is only your thoughts about yourself and the world, the ideas that you choose to believe as truth that determines your experience and forges your own individual view of your life.

"With a mind disturbed by emotion, we are at risk of thoughts, words and actions that may increase the suffering and damage already caused. With a clear mind, we are in a better position to serve and benefit those who are grieving."

17th Karmapa Thaye Dorje

It is true that one day your maw will expire its final breath and you will pass on. As will everything. Why have we decided that this will be such a terrible thing? I know that, for myself, living is holding a certain awareness and acceptance that the world and all life upon it is miraculous, omnipotent and omnipresent regardless of its supposed ephemeral nature. Thus nothing is ever really destroyed; nor is it ever really created. Holding onto the idea that every existence came about because of all existence before it provides an extremely freeing aspect to life. Such as the understanding that your parents alone didn't create you. The entire universe began your creation at the very dawn of time! If it were not for the trees, which absorb the carbon dioxide that we exhale, which provides us with clean and breathable air, your father could not use his lungs to produce oxygen that flowed within his blood, which imbued his weapon the power to begin its purpose. Try wiping that image from your mind! Land is ample and the ground is perfect to build our homes upon. Build a room in that home, made from concrete, which is water, sand and gravel and pop some silk sheets, made by our brothers and sisters, the insect larvae, on a mattress made of cotton and all you need to complete the setting is the moonlight. Then two humans spend some quality time "creating you" and have it in their minds that they somehow own you for the rest of your life.

This is not to cheapen the role and the importance of the parent. The role is vital to the upbringing of the child and to their usefulness to mankind. To raise happy, joyful, inspiring and useful contributions to the human race is not to be sniffed at in the slightest. Yet I believe that where some parents may folly is in their ownership of the child rather than their responsibility to the child. As I stated in chapter one regarding John Arthur Hadfield's essays, the distinction between rules and principles are not to be passed by if we want to imbue a joyful infrastructure to our children. Rules are necessary, children need them and seek them to understand what is appropriate and what is not. Rules allow a child to not become apathetic. But it is the principles that gives the child purpose and it is the parents who lay down these foundations of rules and principles that can be useful to all beings on this planet. To do otherwise would be much more than to do the child an injustice. It is neglectful to its true nature.

Yet we are part of a far wider family than that of our parents and our siblings... They are very precious and I, personally, give thanks for them every day, however, Life itself has a consciousness, whatever name you choose to call it matters less than whether you believe in it or not, it is here and it is alive. When you walk and feel the breeze across your face you are feeling something that you cannot see. You have no doubt in its existence yet you cannot prove it with words. The breeze that caress' your face is a microscopic part of a gargantuan force that is always present in one form or another. As that breeze touches you, a hundred miles away the same breeze touches someone else. There is a constant and continuous transaction occurring at every moment and it is with you, the world around and within you. Sharing cosmic energies and forces until the end of all time and not a moment before.

Benjamin Fairbairn

Belief is Your First Goal

THERE HAS NEVER BEEN A task too great for us to pursue. Not really. If you believe the opposite is true then take a moment to consider the miracle of all life. Sit in wonder and contemplate all that surrounds you that was either born, grown or built that wasn't there before. All things that, without a dream and a belief in that dream, would not be here today. Believing that you cannot and accepting limitations is a refusal to accept what you already intrinsically know, due to a failure to investigate what you believe to be limitations to your own human nature to survive and thrive.

Limitation comes from a belief system that is within us, placed there by others before us and adopted by us without investigation. When we were babies, we were far too young to question and had no previous experience to inform us that anything might have even been questionable. Questions that could have revealed that limitation and potential is not at all real and belief is the primary catalyst for all subsequent movement. If belief in the movement doesn't exist then neither does the movement itself. Look around you, at all things surrounding you and see what is actually possible that wasn't possible until somebody *believed* that it was. How many things do you use with regular nonchalance with no knowledge nor interest of the deeper intricacies of its mechanism? For how many years have you used a gizmo with confidence only to realise, much later, of a further function you didn't know it had? You can add your own body and mind to this list for, as we may walk around within our skin and our thoughts, we have little to no inkling of the miraculous functions we can perform and inspire. If we did, who knows of the heights we would reach?

If you ever find that your dream is not coming true, it will not be because of its impossibilities, it would simply be because you don't believe in it enough. If at all. If you can convince yourself that it is real on an emotional level then it will begin to be so. The trick is to convince yourself that it is possible in spite of the evidence and then cultivate regardless. Regardless of lack, regardless of circumstance and regardless of disheartenment. This is really all I did to forge my own path and things have been consistently improving with every day. Everything that was ever needed to create the telephone or the car has always been in existence. It was only when possibilities stacked upon each other over hundreds of years that somebody had the idea to do something about it. It began with an idea, then the belief that the idea could become a reality. That's really all there is to it.

Those who create something new only really create a new belief within themselves that something previously unbelievable can be achieved. Everything is always already here. Limitation exists only within oneself and one's own programming.

Who is Holding You Back?

BURROW DEEP AND CHALLENGE YOURSELF to really recognise the details of your programming. Have you a success mentality or one of failure? Do you respond to life's challenges with a mind-set geared towards solutions or is yours focused upon the problem? Failures exist within even the simplest of ventures and must be experienced to determine what works and what does not. Therefore the cause of our detriment is not our failures but our own personal responses to them. Life offers to us lessons and conundrums that only ever become failures when we decide that they are so. Amidst all of your failures there has been one common denominator and that is you. Have you been the one who has been secretly sabotaging your own life all along?

There is a phenomenon. It is an idea and a dis-belief in our ability to handle our own existence and time that has been flowing through humanity for centuries. Human-kind, regardless of upbringing or class, will always seek an authority to follow. Where we find this authority and the cut of its ilk is testament to the type of programming that has been set within the subconscious-mind. Submitted for your own dissection: A young man, thinking highly of a popular American gang "The Crips" exalted the outlaws and stated it as his dream to become a member. He saw them as his trusted brethren; his family, even though he had only ever met but one of them. He projected allegiance to whatever agenda they chose and put himself forward for a multiple-choice initiation. Although none of the choices were pleasant he chose: "survival". This meant he had to endure a beating by four or more of his "brothers" lasting a few minutes so they could *test* what kind of a value he could offer in a fight. He stepped into the local playground and into a group of waiting young men who promptly surrounded him. Suddenly he was struck to the side of the head from behind by a fist intended to cause damage and trauma which was followed by another and another. Others joined in and his head bounced to-and-fro like a ping-pong ball in a tornado. His eye popped and his brain rattled and finally the initiation was over. Amidst cries of "welcome home nigger!" this young man, clearly traumatised, bloodied and dis-orientated, had *chosen* his path. Now he had only to live with it. Back at home he spoke of the ordeal with pride; "I didn't lose nothing from that..." he slurred, wiping the blood from his cracked eye, "... I gained walking away a better man. *I love my brothers*, they did what they had to do". Previous to this moment he stated blame to the area he lived and grew up in and the fact that his sister was killed in a drive-by shooting. He decided that he will always be in danger regardless of whether he was in a gang or not and decided that joining a gang, a "brother-hood" was a far better option for protection. In order to "protect" himself he would now, on a regular basis, endanger and inflict pain in the lives of others with unflinching allegiance. Why would a young man with all of life ahead of him, with the ability to fly, drive, run or walk away from a dangerous situation, walk seemingly of his own accord straight into one? Perhaps it was the fear of death, of the unknown or an ignorance that another way was possible? An ignorance to the idea that the deeper one digs, then naturally the deeper one gets. It could also be the ignorance that his life is impartial and that hope is created by our own actions rather than the hopelessness created by what *others* do to you. Life *can* become hopeless if you dig yourself in so deep that you can no longer see the way out. Would this mean that the exit is no longer there or that it has become too far away to begin to reach towards it? Believing that our time is short almost makes us question the point of even being here in the first place but understanding that our time is precious compels us to utilise it constructively. It could also be the belief that in joining a gang that they are biding by some sort of "warrior code". A way of life that they are to live by as "soldiers"; "warriors". The samurai were warriors and are hailed and revered today as some of the greatest that ever walked the Earth and they too held a code: the "Hagakure" or; "Bushido": The Way of the Samurai, the sixth book of which is dedicated to compassion and courage and states clearly that *"It is evident through old and new examples that samurais with only courage, but without compassion, become extinct."* For the warrior everything is balance. Courage sans compassion is imbalance thus ineffective. True warriors throughout the history of mankind, instead of the cowardice exemplified by gangs and factions that stalk and torment others, have strived to embody honesty, bravery and duty which all are balanced by compassion.

"Be gentle-men, but carry a big stick."

Hanshi Peter Browne –

Founder-Fighting-arts of Great Britain

As for my own personal learnings with regards to compassion I can say with the utmost honesty that it was indeed the last thing on my mind, it actually was not even up for the slightest contemplation, and it took looking beyond my own self-induced therapies in order to gain its vital power.

Benjamin Fairbairn

Compassion

IN THE MIDST OF THE frenzied maelstrom of suffering we are struck by many shrapnel and debris, pulverizing us with incredible velocities; drawing blood from old wounds and opening some anew as no part of us is spared from the vicious onslaught. These shrapnel and debris attack with such frequency and ferocity that there is little space for contemplation of such things like compassion. The debris carry names like the eviscerating hate and the cancerous resentment and the shrapnel is abundant with the ravenous revenge and the unforgiving blame. All these sufferings leave their mark and before we can gather breath we are struck again and again. Sometimes it is all we can do to close our eyes. Below and far away, within this cyclone, we are swept from the ground that stabilises us. The foundation that is called compassion.

There is something that we seek when possessed by anger that compels us to forego things that will create for us the means to happiness and peace and it is aided by the aforementioned shrapnel and debris. Each is a poison and a bewitchment that can cloud the mind and saturate a heart until even its own survival is of no vital importance. *I* wanted to live however I *also* wanted to die. Living was a dream akin to swimming through the cosmos to a vacation on the moon yet the reality that I had created for myself was of a consistent misery and a search for some kind of meaning. That meaning seemed to lay within the purpose of others and I was nothing but a bystander; a spectator to my own story which was being ghost written by the many others who were simply passing through. I had the journals and the poems. I had the music and the martial-arts, I had the drinking and the violence. What were these things other than therapeutic and how did they serve me and, having served me, why was I still so violently miserable?

Catharsis is the greatest ally to misery and is the dominant ingredient to its perpetuation. It is the shot of heroin in the speckled vein of the addict who feels momentary release from a hellish existence only to shudder back to that same reality minus the power to even think to fight for life. In my own catharsis I re-created myself as a devilish fiend. I held an artillery of suffering that other sufferers understood, thus I shared, and this gave me a feeling of importance. Perhaps this is who I was supposed to be? An ambassador of suffering for those who have also suffered. Neither seeking nor curious of another way, being much too bound in comfort by their misery, but seeking instead, a new addition to their communication of that suffering. Catharsis is brotherhood. It is a white picket-fence that surrounds the house of pain and gives a platform to suffering, an auditorium with no back-door thus, once entered, leaving makes little sense. I hated my life. Yet I began to love hating my life.

Hate is demanding and resentment is intrusive. My own hate and resentment left space for nothing more in the quest for answers as to why the child that I once was, was made to suffer with such abandonment. It consumed and sandblasted my thoughts, my dreams, my words and my deeds. I was marinating in hate and it was compassion that freed me from hates confines. I am not ashamed to say that I felt hate towards my father for the treatment that I allowed to later shape my life. Compassion released my own life from the dirge of blame to life and freedom.

With the ferocious accumulation of hate, blame, misery and resentment and with a catharsis to bind them all together, how can anyone hope to break free? How can we hope to calm the storm long enough in order to bring ourselves back to land on the stability of the ground?

Imagine a fighter in the ring whose confidence is stolen by an unending flurry of jabs to the face. In the ring the fighter continues to move forward, hands up, because that is what fighters do, and tries to counter yet, the jabs are too rapid and plentiful. Piece by piece the fighter is jabbed to cuts and with each small hit is rendered hopeless. The fighters "soul" depletes and the will to fight becomes less and less until it is over. The hands drop to the side and the face stays still as a sacrificial offering for the taking until the towel is mercifully thrown in. There is a saying in world of combat that "if you can't knock them out then bleed them out." This is the nature and the danger of catharsis. The jabs seem too small to react to and the danger goes unnoticed until it is too late and all efforts seem futile. It steals away the foresight of what is necessary to break free and what *is* necessary to break free from the flurry of destruction is the powers that lay in compassion and clarity.

Compassion is a magical energy whose power is completely masked by ridicule and misconception yet it is a ground-breaking force that, once harnessed, has an unequalled ability to break the destructive cycle of hate, rage and resentment. Have you ever seen an angry person utilise compassion? One dissolves the other.

How can I possibly suggest compassion in the place of hate? Would this mean to suggest that we could feel compassion for those who have done us wrong and who has caused us harm? To be compassionate to those we have deemed the most hated? I do. Compassion is the pathway to freedom from the confines of hate.

To hate is to dedicate negative energy to; and in order to give this energy life it first needs to be cultivated within your body's own energy and this is expensive. When in the throes of hate the heart is filled with something that feels like passion and excitement and it happens very quickly. Hate perpetuates rapidly and is easily fortified. Hate inside the heart is a fire that sufferers are very accustomed to and its release relies upon a huge valve that is easy to find, fun to turn and releases the built up pressure which locks away our serotonins. Serotonins released, the brain is overcome with an array of feel-good drugs but the muscles in the body, the blood in the veins, the organs and the spirit is left poisoned. Weakened and agitated. The protective nature of the body is worn down and gives way to outbreaks of illness in these places. The places of the blood, the places of the flesh and organs and of the spirit.

The body and the mind and the spirit were born to love and to perpetuate goodness and, regardless of the programming that one was raised with, if uncongenial to its natural purpose, the body, mind and spirit is left to suffer in dis-ease.

Compassion is cultivated but does not come easy as, at first, you must clean away all of the debris that has left the pathway littered with confusion from the cyclone of chaos. I do now have a method of unleashing immediate compassion if my perception decides that someone has wronged me. I focus on their philtrum. The philtrum is the finger-tip sized depression just under the nose and above the lip that has no apparent function but the one that I have created for it. An extremely important function, the philtrum was once fused to the nasal septum during our embryonic development. As the development continued these two began to separate to the dent which we have today. In Jewish mythology, an angel is said to be sitting with us during the embryonic stages, keeping our company and teaching us all the secrets of the universe. Just before we were born into the world, the angel presses a finger to our lip; "Shhhhhhₕₕ ..." and swears the infant "us" to secrecy. Eventually, with all the influence of the world, the great secrets of the universe become forgotten. Focusing on the philtrum is an immediate reminder to me, regardless of the age or ferocity, arrogance or depravity, that we are all tiny miracles that have just forgotten the great secrets that we were taught. That we were all once tiny babies with the world at our feet.

Compassion is a tiny face in the crushing crowd of the many and must actively be sought and meticulously fed in order to be sustained. This means that, as abundant as compassion is, it is as hard as is the reason for trying to find it in the first place. To find compassion among the masses of negativity is a pointless task to be forced. It must be an endeavour of passion and meaning.

"The quality of mercy is not strained, it droppeth as the gentle rain from heaven."

William Shakespeare

In the past I have pursued answers from those who I believed had wronged me, treated me unfairly or abused their position over me and I did this for a great and timely period of my life. If I couldn't find answers or they were forever unavailable to me I instead embraced rage, visceral and intoxicating. It was only when I found that my "wrong-doers" were simply executing their own choices in their own lives and that I had been caught up in the effects of *their* causes that I began a second thought. I felt that I needed to know why but it was more than curiosity. It was *closure*. Without closure my body ached with the need for rectification or punishment. My life and everything in it at the time was wrong and I felt that I had to have *answers* from somebody as to *why*. Somebody needed to be held responsible. Closure would have given me, in my perspective, the answers that I needed. The one who I could hold *responsible*. Moving on was not even a thought that I could entertain. I just had too many questions that needed answering.

One evening, whilst sitting in the bath, I was reading a book by Thich Nhat Hanh named: *"Reconciliation"* and my heart broke into a thousand pieces. It was here that this once and former darkling first experienced the idea of compassion and new, freeing possibilities arose within me. He spoke of the endless cycle of suffering and that running away from the suffering only prolongs it. He spoke of listening with compassion, not only to others but also to the wounded child inside of us. As I sat in the bath I closed my eyes and brought quiet to my soul and when I opened them my child-self was sitting there with me. Facing me. I sat, wrinkling, for a further hour conversing with him, listening and assuring him that I loved him. That I knew he had been hurt and that he had suffered and that he didn't have to suffer any more. That he could stay with me until he could feel happy enough to be free. I learned that compassion meant to understand that my abusers were also children once and had suffered also and had expressed that suffering onto me because they didn't learn any other way to be. And that wasn't my fault. I could see that the child was still suffering now because I had perpetuated his suffering. By holding onto anger and rage I perpetuated his fear and isolation. In my obsessive pursuit for closure I had neglected my own wellbeing. I had neglected myself.

I began to realise that the people I felt had done me wrong had many qualities of good and that the things that hurt me were the reflections of torture that was eviscerating them from within and that they had suffered so strongly that they had no way to express this other than to hurt me. It did not excuse them in any way but it showed me that whatever had happened to me, I was continuing to do to myself. Neglect, physical and mental abuse. I was perpetuating it unconsciously against the child within and, as I sat, I felt compassion flowing through me freely, like a sunbeam, and I felt alive. I came to see that my responsibility lay with my *own* conduct and my own ability to choose healthier ways to live. And theirs was the same responsibility.

"No written word, no spoken plea; can teach our youth what they should be.
Nor all the books on all the shelves; it's what the teachers are themselves."

Anon

46

Accountability

BUT ISN'T IT EXTREMELY IMPORTANT to hold people accountable for their actions? Should not the villains of the world; the murderers and the abusers, the dictators and the warlords be held to account for their terrible pursuits? And what of those who've done wrong to *us*? Who holds them accountable if it is not our responsibility to do so? Who is there to make sure that they receive the effect that is the consequence of their actions?

What does it mean to you to hold somebody accountable for their actions? Take a real moment to ask yourself this and then listen to your answer. Write it down on a piece of paper and then, if necessary, jot down all those you hold accountable for the things that you haven't achieved in life for whatever reason that may be.

There is a common conception with regards to accountability within society and that is its blurred partnership with that of consequence but let's remember that we are speaking of the high performance reflex; about going higher than common acceptance and deeper than a common conception that has been adopted by the mass majority. We are talking about moving away from the victimhood of blame and toward personal power and one of the things that can elevate us to new levels of a greater life is the real power that can be discovered in the accepting of our own responsibility in our lives.

Thus is the other side of the coin; that accountability does not mean consequences nor does it exist in relation to negativity. We have tied this powerful word to mean something that lives alongside a negative consequence. When we think of holding someone accountable for their actions can we honestly think of a positive example or is it purely something we have filed under punishment and consequence.

I make the argument for the other side of the coin because it is a power that was pivotal to my progress and was one of the most fundamental factors that dissolved the excuses I was creating to account for the failures in my own life. I say that accountability is power and I say that not without recognition of the gravity that the opposing belief holds.

Accountability is a purely personal recognition and it is the freedom from pain to peace. It is recognising the power that we have in our lives and the power to alter and effect our outcomes. It removes from us the victimhood of blame and stands us squarely on the precipice of power. Accountability is the power of personal responsibility for our actions *and* the acceptance of the consequences they bring. In short; accountability addresses the changes that we are responsible for making in our lives. And that responsibility belongs to none but the beholder.

Submitted for your perusal: Somebody has committed a wrong-doing to you and to society and harbours not a single regret for their actions. They have acted in a way that is unacceptable to society and they do not care, so society holds them accountable. Then what? Now that we have held them accountable for their actions what would we like them to do? Or what would we like to do to them? Is punishment accountability?

In his best-selling book, Blink; Malcolm Gladwell states that "It is really only experts who are able to reliably account for their reactions". So what does this mean? Does it suggest that we actually can't hope to be accountable for our actions unless we're experts of some sort? The example that was shared was based on an experiment that sought to find the best strawberry jam available. Forty-four different brands of strawberry jam were given to a team of expert food tasters who ranked them according to taste and texture. Once they had been ranked, five of the jams were given to a group of college students to test how close the student's rankings came to the expert rankings. "The answer is, pretty close" Says Gladwell. The difference in results between the college students and the experts were minimal and the results were almost identical. It would seem that expertise could be considered as over-rated, if the experiment were to end there. That is not where the experiment ended however. When given a questionnaire to explain the specific reasons for their reactions and judgements towards the jams, to account for their choices, it was only the experts who could determine exactly why they chose the way they did. The students had no idea why (or, no idea how to articulate why) they had made the choices that they did even though their results were extremely close to the expert results. The expert tasters, however, did not suffer the same limitations. They knew exactly how to articulate their results, what they had tasted and why they had made the choices they did. This is quite an experiment for a number of reasons. The main one being that it highlights the confusion that stems from ignorance. The other thing it highlights is that frustration and anger can stem from an inability to articulate our actions, choices and even how we feel about things, which is not a bad thing despite how it sounds. It is the reason why we love poetry and music and stories. Someone always has an ability to capture our sentiments and articulate it in a new and beautiful way to which we can relate.

This is a great revelation and it can also help us to incentivise our intentions. If your motivation is to seek excuses for the lack of personal achievements, excuses for the difficulty you experience in life and your contentment in this world then look no further. These findings can provide the seekers of the excuse; the victims, the perfect proof that they cannot be accountable for their own cause and effect as nobody can be experts in everything. It can indicate that we don't have to be accountable because we simply can't be experts in everything life related. The excuse finders will indeed look no further as they possibly believe that they can never be experts.

An expert, however, is not somebody who knows everything about a subject in particular. It is an individual who seeks to inform themselves. A jam expert does not know everything about jam. If that was the case we'd have the perfect jam and there would be no need for improvement of any kind. This enlightened jam guru would give teachings on the perfect jam and all other jams would become obsolete. Seeing as that has never happened on any subject whatsoever it is fair to say that experts are people who action a vast interest in compiling, as thorough and accurate the information and proof as they can, develop informed theory and seek to challenge the limitations of their own knowledge. So to those who seek to excel their human performance in this life, this strikes as fantastic news to behold! If we wish to be more successful in and take ownership of our actions and their effect on our lives, we would then strive to be more comprehensive as to our motivations so that our actions are no longer confusing to us. In order to be an expert of ourselves, I put out the idea that, all we would have to do would be to strive in becoming more interested in ourselves and the life surrounding us and to gain some intention as to what we want to do and where we would like to be. Even on the most basic level. The expert in you would then work to manifest that intention consciously and purposefully. Creating a more accountable and purposeful living being.

There are those of us who, for one reason or another, simply do not have the ability to question their motivation or to understand their intentions. There are those who simply cannot, at the time, articulate or understand their actions. There are also those who perform acts that abuses the greater good of mankind and it is in these conditions that we can hold these people to account. It is important to understand, however, that when we decide to hold someone to account, it is to ourselves that we foster the responsibility for that person or persons in their stead. Holding someone to account is holding onto and adopting responsibility for that person or act. A judge who holds a felon to account for their actions means that they will be locked up in a prison for which the authorities are responsible for. This person cannot be trusted to command ownership of their actions so the powers that be foster that responsibility. Such is the same of the parent who is accountable for the child until the child is old enough to hold their own account.

This is also a great revelation for those of us who are having a hard time letting go. To realise that holding to account those who have harmed us and committed wrongs against us, means to foster; to temporarily *hold* within ourselves, the responsibility for those people until they realise their folly and thus, return responsibility back to their own hands.

If a crime has been committed, it makes sense that the responsibility would be to the legal authority to exact some kind of balance, be that of therapy or punishment. Yet if someone has done us wrong, it would be unsound to foster the responsibility for another as holding another accountable can be a life-long bane as they may never realise their folly, leaving you to hold their burden, along with your all of your own, for as long as you live. Understanding cause and effect can allow us to let go from holding onto other people's responsibilities for their life choices and actions and allow us the vast horizons to explore with freedom and freshness. Professional therapy is highly advisable in finding ways of allowing ourselves to be free of this so that the real joy of life can begin.

The word accountability would serve much greater a purpose if we raise it from the bogs of negative consequence and reclaim the real power it holds within our own journey. I believe that we may *recognise* what somebody has done, right or wrong, and we may *expect* them to take responsibility and to do what is considered "the right thing to do." Whether they do it or not is completely their own responsibility. I claim that when we "hold somebody accountable" for their own actions what we are actually also doing is holding some kind of *hope* that they will do what is expected of them. Ultimately, what they end up feeling, doing or believing is a journey only they can take. We can always choose to *support* somebody along their journey but the power of accountability is all their own and our own. We are all running on the track and we all have our own hurdles to clear. By focusing on somebody else's race we run the risk of tripping on our own. We can run beside them while we make our own leaps and bounds and offer words of support but we cannot take the responsibility of the race away from them. They will choose their own way. Enforcing what we expect on to somebody does nothing to change what they think or feel. Our expectancy may even prove to be the distraction that trips them and hinders their journey.

Support and mentoring on the other hand, may affect them to understand another way to approach the situation and it may give them an opening to understand a harmful action but the responsibility to make that change lays firmly with the individual.

As individuals we may be held accountable by many and so many more all coming at us with so many different perspectives of many different things. How then do we choose which the right perceptions are and which ones, the wrong? What should we do to satisfy and pacify all those who hold us accountable and where does it all end? Cause and effect is very real and it is very personal to the individual. Isaac Newton's third law states that: "*for every action there is an equal and opposite reaction.*" Cause and effect exists without discrimination and it is the same for all beings on the planet. For all living things that move and breathe. As humans we feel compelled to hold others accountable for their actions. We may know of someone's actions and it may affect us deeply, yet it is them that has effected a cause and it is them they who will cause an effect in their own lives. It is up to you what you do with yours and this is a super power. The power to take back all the actions that occur within your life. The mesmeric world of blame or "holding to account" can lead us to forget that we hold a power to affect change in our lives that can influence and inspire others to make changes within theirs. This power is always ready to surge.

The consequences of our actions are coming whether we are held to them by others or not.

Accountability is recognising free will and ownership of our actions and being prepared to reap the fruits of those actions. Holding someone accountable is force-feeding them a fruit that you believe they should be eating.

"Accountability is the realisation that the quality of my choices determines the quality of my life."
Brian P. Moran- Author- The 12 Week Year

And what of closure? What is it, why do we feel that we need it and when are we satisfied that we have it? Closure is answers that have actually nothing to do with us at all. Closure is wanting to know why someone else's suffering has affected upon us more suffering and why it continues to do so. We seem to want these answers in the hope that this knowledge will somehow satisfy us and stop the suffering but the opposite is almost always the case. When we discover why we were made to suffer it hurts more and we become even more confused. The answer is also painfully sought and by looking towards others we find ourselves missing the point. We already have the answer. The reason someone else's suffering continues to affect us is because we allow it to by refusing to let go and compassion is the power that allows us to let go. Not for the sake of our persecutors but for our own progress in life. Letting go is freeing your body from the belief that it must labour in the production of poisonous emotions within itself. The need to produce and harbour poisons in your heart and mind that eventually bring you to your knees. I know only too well that, in order to inflict rage and hate upon another, it must first be charged within your own vessel and this does not have a menial effect therein. Among other things, the arteries constrict whilst the blood pumps harder and faster causing physical pain to the one who hates. Why does a broken heart hurt so much?

When we release this responsibility of the wrong that has befallen us and the need for closure as to why this wrong happened in the first place, we become unbound, free and powerful. The warrior understands the power of compassion and realises the bravery, resilience and awareness that is needed to utilise it to allow us to stand inside our destiny. That, despite experiencing a past that failed in laying a beneficial road ahead, we can begin by laying that road ourselves. Brick by brick. And we can begin right now.

The Possibility of Dreams Made Manifest

INSIDE MOST WOMEN ARE MILLIONS of immature eggs, miniscule and miraculous and once a month, one will grow to maturity to escape the others where it then travels down the fallopian tubes. This egg sits for twenty-four hours awaiting the next stage of miraculous happenings, however if this does not occur, the egg disintegrates and its journey ends where another is released to take its place. This cycle continues until the egg is fertilised by the seed of man and another miraculous stage begins thence forth – the beginning of a single human life. The sperm-cell that meets the egg is the lucky one. The others all die as they are dissolved within the acidic nature of the protective immune system as they are viewed as foreign bodies and are destroyed.

Imagine a swimming contest of a quarter-billion competitors on one side and the trophy of Life on the opposite end of the pool. On either side of this pool are the protectors armed with spears, machine-guns and cauldrons filled with acids and boiling liquids prepped for pouring upon all who enter the pool. These protectors have one sole purpose: to stop any one from gaining access to the other side and obtaining the prize. At the sound of the bang a quarter-billion competitors rush into the waters, fighting and clambering over one another and, once in the pool, they are systematically slaughtered. Some have little chance as they are either poor swimmers or abnormally formed but the others fight. Through the slaughter they strive and push. Through rigid determination they fight and die and through it all - only one out of the quarter-billion takes the prize.

That one is every single one of us.

When was the last time that we had to fight against the odds of a quarter of a billion in a stake of life and death? Where we had to race against time lest we be burned from existence? Why would you allow the last time you fought with all your might for your goal and your right to be alive, be when you were but a sperm? You were born with an innate goal striving mechanism. You had it at the beginning of life and you have it now. Over time we have been conditioned to forget that we are destined to strive to be alive and to prosper. We forgot the whisperings of the angels. We have accepted the conditioning that allowed us to believe that we are mediocre beings destined for mediocre things to a mediocre end yet that is not the case. We are fighters by our nature. Hunters who strive and survive. It is what you believe that compels you to behave otherwise.

Today and all around we can hear the woes of how difficult and how pointless life is when in fact, and by actual definition, we are all living miracles with a unique opportunity to impact this world and our lives with greatness. We were all born winners. Winning was our first achievement and today we have become crushed and flaccid when we are denied permission by others, in monetary lack or if our partner leaves us for someone else. Why have we allowed ourselves to become mired in mediocrity when our nature and our innate greatness is to be bursting with unlimited potential? Can you not feel it within you? The greatness vibrating just beneath the surface waiting for the order to burst forth and affect your life forevermore?

Human potential is limitless. I believe that as children we are aware of this. As we grow into adolescence we become more aware instead of the pressures of time causing us to forego our potential for the lack of knowing where to begin. We get caught up in the acceptance or neglect of our reflections. In the world accepting us in one way or another. The key lies in intention and choice. To choose an aspect of your potential that you can focus on and to bring it to useful fruition through enjoyment. Time is plentiful and there will be opportunities that build more opportunities. The key is focus, intention and action.

The first thing we must be aware of, if we are ever to *truly live* in this world, is that the world we create for ourselves is the sum total of our very own thoughts and *not* of our potential.

Benjamin Fairbairn

The Realms of Thoughts and Thinking

IF IT IS SO THAT we are the sum total of our thoughts than this must also mean that our lives are the sum totals of our thinking. If we delve deeper into the realms of thoughts and thinking, in what causes it to occur and what we have been confusing for thinking all this time, perhaps we can begin to create a brand new method of thinking that can create new opportunities for our lives. Not all activity occurring within the conscious mind is thought, although it is commonly mistaken as such. The conscious mind is effervescent with activity of all sorts of things which is mostly arbitrary bushwah; songs we hate that won't leave our heads, what this person thinks about that and that person about this and all sorts of nonsense as such. *Thought*, however, is a *skill* of the mind and like all skills, must be cultivated, shaped and practiced in order to become strong and intentional. Unconscious "thought" is something else entirely. It is a reactionary process that serves very little purpose most of the time and no purpose the rest of the time. *Conscious* thought is a very sophisticated skill and here is why; the conscious mind, although it is capable of all of its intellectual factors as well as the ability to choose, is still governed by the programming *within the sub-conscious mind*. The sub-conscious mind in turn, for all its unlimited power, is the product of the unconscious contribution of others. All sorts of others who were not necessarily masters of mind-programming.

Without constant vigilance, *everything* that we do may be governed by something other than our own wishes. Our results, in turn, are manifesting as outcomes we are not familiar with and our lives become a product of unconscious contribution that we are confused by. Our bodies, rather than fulfilling its ability to create anything it may dream of, reacts moment by moment to anxieties of the future or past happenings of regret and nostalgia both dragged, confused - kicking and screaming from their rightful homes to a present moment where they don't belong. A present moment which in turn is forgotten, neglected and ultimately becomes that wasted opportunity to impact a unique brilliance upon this world.

However, as it is always easier to judge outwardly, why not take a look at our own family. The next time we are at a family meal or just go to pay a visit, take heed to the activities of the mind our loved-ones engage in. Watch for thought patterns that seem a little funky. A little aimless. Note the frequency. Now pay extra attention to a mind of even more consequence. Keep track of your own thoughts. Where have your own beliefs and ideas about life stemmed from? Do you truly agree with the things you acclaim or are you just going with the flow? This is not an exercise to put you, your family or anyone else on trial, it is simply an exercise in being aware where your mind is and what it is producing for you. After all, if it is true that we become what we think about, it would be nice to be aware of what we are becoming.

"Every day stand guard at the gates of your mind."

Jim Rohn

Why We Are Limitless

LIFE AND OUR ABILITIES ARE completely and utterly limitless. It may seem ridiculous to suggest so, yet take for a moment the scenario of yourself as a fly on the wall in a small room with two people (a man and a woman) as an argument begins to smoulder. This argument escalates to quite a heated situation where violence breaks out. Glasses are thrown, broken against a wall and a table is over-turned. Try to imagine the volume and the energy that must fill this room. How does it feel? Try to picture it as a colour. What is the colour? Is it a soft, misty cyan or a deep and heavy red? Now, the argument dies down. The glass is cleaned up and the furniture is placed upright. Everything looks just as it did before the fallout, but that energy is still there, creeping through the entire room. You see someone else enter and look around, everything seems to be in order but they too can feel it, this negative energy. The occurrence taken place in that room has left an imprint. It has affected the people within the room and anyone else that may enter. In the minds of the people in the room the significance is all consuming even though it was a fallout in just a small room. Somewhere else in the world an invasion occurs on a large scale and many innocent people are abused and slaughtered. This energy is felt all across our planet as the world reacts in anger and mourns its sympathy. Its people create charities and songs and protests against the inhumanities. The entire world over can feel the significance, heavy, like a planetary heartbeat... ... Up in the great vastness of space, deep in the blackness and among the multitude of stars and moons, scattered within the infinite, our planet Earth, through all its wars and devastations, through the cries and woes, cracks, shatters, crumbles and implodes into insignificance... Now there is silence absolute. And all the while, the great infinite, deep in the forever, continues on and barely even notices our demise. Its agenda remains and its cosmic intelligence doesn't even blink to mourn...

This is not neglect, it is focus.

The greatest problem we can think of, the greatest dream we find impossible, is nothing that hasn't been thought of, dreamed of or experienced already a thousand times over.

How can anything be impossible to us when the entire Universe is moving around us supporting our existence? Even the most brilliant thoughts are only discoveries of what the infinite has always known. Of what already is. There is nothing really amazing occurring in our discovery, what is *actually* amazing becomes our *awareness* of what is occurring within the Universe. It is *only ever* the awareness. Nothing is created that was not already there, in some form, in the first place. We simply discover the recipe using ingredients that have always existed. The discovery is not as new as our awareness and experience of it. Thus our goals, aims and aspirations are nothing new, they are nothing unachievable, we must simply discover the laws of their acquisition and move accordingly along those lines. It is like the fact that your partner was somewhere in existence before you met them and when you met, your experience of them began. Viktor Frankl, in his study: Man's Search for Meaning, had this to say on this matter; "The only really transitory aspects of life are the potentialities; but as soon as they are actualized, they are rendered realities at that very moment." In his book: The 12 Week Year, Brian P. Moran says this regarding moving along those said lines, "It's not enough to have a vision and a plan. If your goals and plans are designed to help you achieve a higher level of performance, then you most likely have specific tactics that are new actions for you. New actions are almost always uncomfortable. That's one of the things that makes change so difficult. It's one thing to identify the actions needed to create a better result; it's a whole other thing to consistently do them."

As much as this world and all of its miracles are here and ready for us to experience, it takes many of us a lifetime to begin (and many of us end our lives without ever) opening our minds to become available to accept what our world has to offer and once we do, finding the strength and cultivating the discipline to do what must be done becomes a whole new challenge where new skills and habits must be developed and a belief that it can be done is imperative to their acquisition.

Benjamin Fairbairn

.

Altered States

*Those who are devoid of spiritual perception are unable to
recognise anything that cannot be seen externally.*
—Paracelsus

AMAN IS TAKEN TO A cabin, off grid, in the woods. In the cabin there is a
larder that is full with food and water to last him through the month and he
is left there alone to fend for himself. There are no locks on the door or the
windows, leaning against one of the wood-beamed walls is a loaded rifle...
As the end of the month draws closer, the man realises that he will soon run
out of all sustenance. He continues to eat until the food and water finally and
completely depletes. The man looks around the small wood cabin for more,
but finds none. He takes up his rifle, steps out onto the porch as he looks
around intently. He gently closes his eyes and focuses his ear to the
wilderness. He lifts his chin a tad and inhales deeply through his nostrils but
he cannot detect anything useful. Not a scrap nor crumb. Not a drip nor
dribble. He ventures back inside the cabin and opens again the larder. Still
no food. So he returns to the porch and sits, rifle in hand, breathes deep a
sigh and waits. He contemplates his life day after day and night after night,
reminiscing on days gone by, until he is gradually attacked by the pain of a
clenching and cramping hunger - alone until finally he lays down to sleep
and never again wakes. What is the first thing that strikes you about this tale
of the man in the wood cabin? Is it sadness at his death? Confusion as to why
he was left there or who it was who left him? Of course it's not. My guess is
that you are wondering why he didn't venture out to the woods to hunt or
forage for more food and water? Does it not seem like that would be the first

thing to do? So why didn't he? Why would he simply succumb to a death without even trying to live? The answer is simple. The man couldn't *see* any more food. He couldn't see any animals to hunt, he couldn't see any vegetables growing from the ground. He couldn't hear any water flowing nor smell any food nearby. There was no obvious sign nor guarantee that there was anything for him beyond the small cabin so he waited for something to come to him, rifle in hand. Ready to strike. This sounds obviously ridiculous yet, as obviously ridiculous as it is, is this not what so many are guilty of in today's world? How many people do you know who are living in that small wood cabin? Sitting and waiting for everything to come to them? Waiting for proof of the existence of something else before they can step off of their porch and even try to live? It sounds ridiculous yet the man in the cabin is an analogy of a reality that so many of us are living with in every single day of our lives. Living within the safety of convenience even though it is slowly killing them. Unsure of a purpose to life. Sitting in front of the TV and video game attempting to drown out the pleas of our hearts which yearn to be met with life and adventure. How many are ready to judge the man in the cabin for suffering the same wasted chance of life that we too are too frequently guilty of?

Consider there are three states; the state of the physical, the state of the intellect and the state of the spirit. Within the state of the physical lives only what we can sense within our five sense funnels. When the physicality is insufficient to accomplish a certain task or goal or to satisfy explanations, we must move up one level to the intellectual state where what we have learned can support what we see and what we believe – as is the case with the water-cycle. Within the state of the intellect are six factors. These factors are the memory, the intuition, the perception, the imagination, the will and the power to reason. These factors are powerful and can achieve most things our dreams and desires can conjure. Book, academia and experience are utilised to fortify this state and the artillery of these factors are widely sought and revered. Yet some reach the highest heights of the intellect and are still not content as there are some things that the intellect cannot comprehend, and that cannot be taught through book or academia. Some things are also not so easy for experience to recognise. It goes to say then that there are some things even these great powers cannot reach. When this occurs, one must again move up a state to that of the spirit. When all we know has been tried we can stop or we can turn to something greater. An attempt for deeper understanding through submission to a higher power. We cannot see every stage of the water cycle yet, using the power of the intellect we have it within our reasoning that such a thing occurs because that is what we have been taught. But when imagination cannot conjure, when reasoning fails, will is depleted and perception is marred, there is another power that we can tap into. Much like the radio can play many frequencies, we can tap into the frequency that we need when we need it. But these powers are not as simple as turning a dial. Many find the spiritual state in times of despair or desperation. The man in prison may submit to the higher power of religion. The grieving spouse may visit someone who can connect them with their dearly transcended. It is in these times that it is common that we may open up to the spiritual state yet it is always available and can be experienced at any time of life.

Take a pot of water. This pot of water is, at the moment, in a corporeal or physical state and can be proved as such within any of our five physical senses. We can see it, taste it, touch it and hear it sploshing around, although it doesn't smell of much. If this water is heated it bubbles and eventually changes its state from a physical to an astral one and becomes steam. In this state we can still see it, feel it and we can explain how it looks and why it has become this way using our intellect and what we have learned about it from the past. If this continues to heat up it will change state once again from one of an astral nature to that of an etheric nature. It has now become one with the air, ether or gas. Here we have something that cannot be seen nor touched. It is unlikely to be experienced with the physical senses and more challenging to explain using the intellect, thus it becomes simple to discount as being there at all. With the states of water, we know it's there yet we are not sure how we know. We just know because we were taught to know. Cool it down and it begins to alter its state to that of the astral and then again to the corporeal where we can experience it once again at a more comfortable level. A more provable level.

The thing that was being heated was always what we can call water and the states that were being changed as it was heated were its vibratory rate. The water changed frequency at a vibratory level each time and altered its states based on the levels of vibrations the water experienced. Everything vibrates, just at different frequencies at different times. Some things we can see, some things we can explain and some we can do neither.

Take money for example. Money is this thing that we trade for something else, something that we like. It would make sense that; the more we have, the more we can trade for things we like or things we like to do. If we have little or none then it would seem that we can do little or nothing. If we want more then we must work harder and trade more time and more effort for more money so we can trade our money for more things. This is our understanding of money at its corporeal level. The intellectual level of understanding, in terms of the six intellectual factors, is that money is a game that needs to be learned and played. We can study money and math and finance and we can understand the level of commitment necessary in order to attain more money. The spiritual level looks at money as a philosophy. An idea. It is this philosophy that determines how much money we have. Some have the idea that money is good, some say money is evil and some say money is exemplified by what is in our hearts. Neither good nor evil and it is this philosophy that determines the flow of money within our lives. What we believe. We need not understand or actively partake in any of these levels as our sub-conscious programming is always busy doing it for us automatically. Taking care of every motion and notion. We already have our philosophy about money and that is why we either have it or have not. This is the same in our relationships with people and the world around us.

We already have our physical experience with these things, our learned understanding of them and our philosophies regarding their nature. However if we were not satisfied with our experience, knowledge and philosophy we needn't accept it. We can consciously reject our programming. It is possible and it is happening all the time with results that people can't seem to explain as it occurs in a state that doesn't require any verbal language. It turns out that not everything has a word.

In marketing there is the philosophy of the seven Ps. These Ps stand for product, price, promotion, place, physical environment, people and process. The idea is that each of these are planned for with a purpose to create a marketing strategy. If the marketing strategy needs to be altered all that is needed to do is to alter one of the Ps and the whole thing changes. A brand new marketing plan is created and brand new results occur just like that. Sometimes the results work in the company's favour and sometimes not. That is part of the game.

It is much the same with the three states. If our lives are headed into a direction we do not wish for it to be going and feel powerless to stop we can write down on paper what we believe about people and our world on a spiritual, intellectual and physical level, and should we have no idea where these principles have come from or we just don't like the look of them we can begin to make a change in the way we look at these things. As coined by physicist Max Planck; *"when we change the way we look at things, the things we look at begin to change."*

When we begin to make the changes to any of our states we will be required to accommodate the changes with new actions to bring about new results to our life. Change always involves doing things we have never done before and therefore will not be comfortable. Get ready for that. We may feel like children again. As a matter of fact, it is exactly what is happening. When we begin to alter our states of consciousness we are effectively reborn in a different light. The reason we achieved so much as children was because we had not yet developed the sentiment to failure. As children we fail and fail and fail again yet we keep going until we win. There is no embarrassment, shame or fear of judgement. It is only later in our years that failure is learned and developed. Failure becomes a scary thing based or our intellectual view of the world and that is why change becomes so hard when we become older. We create an instant mind-map of all the things that can go wrong and the time it will take and the sacrifices we will have to make, and we quit before we even begin. We don't want to look inadequate.

It takes an intellectual reprogramming to be able to undertake such a task as changing our lives for the better and in order to find the strength and resilience to alter our intellect in turn takes an alteration of our spiritual nature to one that can fortify and galvanise us through our new journey. This is my interpretation of the studies that were conducted by Dr. Thurman Fleet that can be further looked upon in his publication "Rays of the Dawn".

This is about questioning the limiting beliefs we hold about this world. It is about observing ourselves and our behaviour objectively and initiating a process of intentional design that will be beneficial to the many in our future.

Once we realise that our existence is intrinsically tied in with every other existence than we can begin to understand that our possibilities can be endless and we can begin to create what we would truly like to do with our lives. And creation has nothing to do – by the way - with truth. Truth is something completely different. Creation is all about designing a lie that is purposeful and, should you tell yourself more than aplenty that the lie you create is actually so, that lie will begin to manifest itself as belief which eventually will become a truth in your world. Once this happens you can continue to live this lie, which is called "delusion" or, once believed, this "lie" can be worked and cultivated until its manifestation converges into reality. From thoughts to words to deeds. From nothing to something to everything. Believe it.

Look upon the magnificent ocean in all its vastness and see that this is where the multitude of worlds and possibilities collide. The mind of man; a magical manifold of mysteries, gazing with a unique perception across a cavorting, mesmerising sheet of motion as it reflects upon its glistening waves the timeless and infinite depths of space above it, morphed within a gentle rippling, gifted by an uncontained and cool breeze which feeds to the ear a whisper bestowed with cosmic promise. Where have I heard that whisper before?

Albeit we can never hope to gaze upon all of the ocean all at once. We can only see what is within our field of vision and even then we can never hope to see to the great depths in all of its completeness blessed with the great myriad of life which graces each and every fathom. We can only see a section of the surface. So we choose to look at the part that is closest to us and, as we choose, we can take up our hands, a cup or even a bucket, fill it with some of the ocean and do with it as we please. We can create a use for it of our choosing. It can become sustenance or it can extinguish a fire. It can wash our clothes or our hair or indeed we may use our portion to drown someone in and kill them. However, the section we take up is always attached to the ocean vast. It will always be of the ocean. The occupation you have given it has nothing to do with the remaining vastness or its nature, that choice and power was yours, yet, whatever use you chose to imbue this water with, the rest of the ocean will not follow. The ocean remains pure, intelligent and vast. This is the nature of your life and the energy that surrounds us. We are, all of us, the "good" the "bad" and the "ugly" a part of the same un-ending vastness. We are all intrinsically tied to and by something that will never be fully revealed to anyone. What we choose to do with this tiny drop of the infinite is completely up to us. The infinite power will continue to regulate regardless. Thus there is never a goal that is too awesome to achieve, no plan too elaborate to execute and no dream too ridiculous to manifest to reality. The infinite is here and we are a very tiny part of, and paradoxically, a hugely important part of the bigger picture. Thus, it goes to say that the only limitations are the ones we have learned to apply to ourselves. Limitations are not the end but the beginning, however it is the start that stops the majority. Begin your adventure knowing that the world is on your side and that you can arm yourself; either with the perfect reason for failing or with the unending artillery of possibility and power.

Preparation for the Pain/Cultivation of the Master-Skill

ONCE THERE WAS A MAN who happened across a caterpillar's cocoon. He decided to take it home to his desk and watch its transformation into a butterfly. He waited and watched as he worked and one day he noticed activity within the cocoon so he placed it on a piece of paper in front of him and observed through a magnifying glass, the wonderful occurrence before him. Through a tiny hole in the tip of the cocoon he noticed the little life struggling to squeeze through. He saw the being labour arduously yet to no avail and became quite concerned regarding its chance of survival so he took up a scalpel and carefully, lovingly implied a tiny incision at the mouth of the cocoon creating ease for the new life to escape. Pleased with his aid the man excitedly placed the scalpel back and continued to view through the glass. He watched as the being eased out of the cocoon, soaked and bound by the membrane of new life, unable to breath and barely able to move let alone spread its beautiful new wings and fly. It continued to drag itself along the stained mahogany, leaving a trail of ooze behind it. The man watched, helplessly now as the tiny being suffered, asphyxiated and died in front of him.

The following is a controversial statement: suffering can be a most misunderstood necessity of life and sometimes the best of intentions can lead to unnecessary further suffering or worse. There are of course, varying degrees of suffering in life. The paradox of it all is that the more obvious and brutal the suffering the less obvious the necessity and many gurus believe that suffering is not necessary to life at all. I have read varying opinions and my own understanding, through my own experience is this: I believe that suffering is more than just the perception one adopts, it is also the discomfort one feels. Through the discomfort one may adopt a positive countenance and attitude which *may* help them through the difficult situation; an opportunity that they otherwise would not have; allowing them to perceive the issue from a more beneficial angle. This would be an example of the learning through our suffering. Adopt a catharsis or lack of hope when suffering and this creates a free highway for the suffering to travel through the body with no resistance; thus perpetuating the suffering. This would be an example of unnecessary suffering.

"From my earliest recollection, I date the entertainment of a deep conviction that slavery would not always be able to hold me within its foul embrace; and in the darkest hours of my career in slavery, this living word of faith and spirit of hope departed not from me, but remained like ministering angels to cheer me through the gloom."

Frederick Douglas

Frederick Douglas was a man who had every reason to give in to all of his suffering. Slavery had just been abolished and all former slaves were now considered freemen, women and children. These were not all they were, they were all, collectively released without a means to survive. Most were unskilled and had to deal with and try to exist within the stigma of a corrupt society. However, if a man who, on top of all this, was someone who didn't know his Father but knew of him and knew that he was a slave-master and abuser; if this man had ample family all around him living on a plantation, who were bred as stock as which to serve and perish when their usefulness had expired; a man who saw his Grandmother's kind hearted soul, left to die in the middle of a barren forest after a life-time of caring for others, including those who saw her to her doom; who saw his brethren killed and maimed horribly and who suffered torture and abuse daily – if a man such as this can forge such a point of view of strength and compassion in the stead of victimhood and rage, what excuse do we have? I would never chance to minimize the strife that anyone has endured and suffered throughout their lives. I would only venture to put forth the challenge to all to dismiss the allowance of your past or present sufferings to affect or determine your future possibilities. However, struggle is real and, regardless of how much milk has been spilled, if you're are moved to tears by it, who is anyone to tell you that you should not be?

My own expertise stems not from years of academia and book but from a young man who experienced a second and third decade upon this Earth as little more than a seminar of suffering. A being who had no idea as to the whys of his suffering or existence. Of a child who had suffered and within which a deep abscess of hate grew and poisoned him. A suffering that was hidden yet pulsated beneath the façade and threatened to one day make itself known. And the re-emergence from the cocoon of suffering to peace, love and prosperity. My career as a darkling was a long and cathartic suffering and it was with a great and euphoric difficulty that I managed to break free from the encrusted scab of my hateful, fearful and potentially dangerous existence. I did what was confusing and controversial against advice from the tiny devil on my shoulder to fight through the thorned bramble of limitation from which I emerged lacerated and bloody yet fresh, vulnerable and ready to begin a newness of life... And still today I salve those old wounds.

The spectrums for all things that exist takes quite some space to open up and to become aware of. To be aware that the spectrum of experience *begins* with suffering is an important discovery. Even sex for the first time begins with much anxiety. This is the same with every experience regardless of the level of suffering. Somewhere near the end of the spectrum sits wisdom. This patient entity sits and is commonly ever discovered, yet it is always there. Sitting sweetly and content, ready and waiting. So it makes sense to me that to expect success within any journey is to expect a certain amount of difficulty along the way extending to an understanding that the greater the journey the greater then will be the suffering. This may immediately bring thoughts of woe but that is only if the suffering is futile which we know that it doesn't have to be. As mentioned previously, an understanding of the nature of growth is an understanding that the struggle, at least in the beginning of any new undertaking, is a great necessity. Without the knowledge and active understanding of the nature of new growth, the attempt to avoid all suffering is normal. This is achieved through the complete avoidance of growth and challenge altogether. Thus it becomes paramount that we understand that, before we decide to throw ourselves into a daring undertaking, the prize is in direct subsequent to the failure. So how much do you want the prize, if you actually even want it at all?

"Kids, you tried your best and you failed miserably. The lesson is: never try."

Homer Simpson

Conditioning Against the Pain

WHEN MY FATHER WAS A young man, the Bruce Lee era was in full fly-kicking force. Like many, he became bewitched with the skill-set, dynamic movement and the power of martial-arts and so it was everywhere when I was growing up. Movies, books and magazines could be found all around the house and, for my siblings and I, the martial-arts stars of Hong Kong and Japan were far more prominent than that of Hollywood. At a very young age my Father began preparing me to be "tough". He taught me how to condition my fists and my forearms by striking the walls over and over again. He told me to do this often and to repeat whilst I struck; *"it doesn't hurt!"* It did of course yet the more I struck, the less it hurt and eventually I felt nothing but the impact. No pain. I gained pride from swollen and bloody knuckles and soon they became strong. As a teenager I began practicing martial arts in the dojo. I quickly learned that part of the development as a martial artist is not learning techniques and the correct way to do things alone, but to also condition the body so that it can be a real tool for the purpose of defence in a crisis situation. This is something that you can't hope will happen within the critical moment because it won't. Instead it takes steady and deliberate conditioning over a long period of time which is painful and many people, once they feel the pain, see it as unnecessary. They have it in mind that there is no reason for the pain so they perhaps complain and stay. They may decide to continue but to not go so hard, to which end, they may gain belt after belt but they would be useless as a defender. They would be an unconditioned weapon that can be easily broken. Alternatively they may choose to leave. Either way they decided to try to avoid the pain and therefore they would forego the true prize and the ultimate goal that they sought out in the first place. Pain is a good reminder but it can also cause us to forget what is important.

Saying that failure is a necessary aspect of success does little to prepare one for either failure or success. It is like saying that we can tolerate pain. It is a ridiculous notion to think that anybody can tolerate pain as pain only begins when it hurts. If it doesn't hurt then it is not pain. It is still within the spectrum of your tolerance to pain, which is quite different. The pain begins the same moment your tolerance to the pain ends. It may hurt yet it is not the same thing as pain. You may know and understand well that failure and success are on the same spectrum, however, knowing about it achieves absolutely nothing when it really hits. When everything you think can be done has been done and nothing is working, when the bank is dry and the rent is due, knowing will fare you little comfort. Knowing and awareness are two completely different things. There are many things that we think that we "know" that abandon us when the tide is high. It is in these times, if you will fight on regardless, forget your nurture toward failure and be aware for weak links in your resolve, then you will strengthen your fighter's spirit. It is in these moments of trial that we prepare for the fighter that we wish to become in the future. By actually being the fighter today.

The Great Farmer and the Master-Skill

THE GREAT FARMER UNDERSTANDS that there is a period when there is little, that cultivation will bring much and that his tears will not be sufficient to water his crops. The great farmer is aware that if he plants the seed of doubt, suffering will eventually be his harvest. Cultivate regardless of perceived failure. Failure can only truly occur at the very end and until the end there can be no failure. When the farmer gives up on his crops, failure will occur and, where good crops could have been, weeds will grow in their stead. Take care of and tend to the crops every day, in spite of the drought, in spite of the heat, eventually great things will occur. But it will not happen immediately and this is where awareness is key. Weeds are the negativity in the great garden and they need no prompt to flourish. They need no tweaking, no particular weather, no cultivation whatsoever. They grow in the place of conscious cultivation and they are always there, waiting for you to quit so they can push through.

As does pain, failure too hurts. And weeds constantly await. Cultivate regardless and be aware that no one nor no-thing can inflict upon your garden anything that you do not invite upon it.

To cultivate regardless of the results is the master-skill yet as human-beings we rely on consistent rewards and immediacy. Signs to tell us that we are doing well and that what we are doing is worthy. Signs to let us know that we are doing well is important to incentivise our principles yet these signs are not always so obvious and immediate. This is an illusion created by those around us when we were children. To incentivise our growth we were rewarded immediately and, although I can understand the benefits in instant rewards for a child, it is definitely not how nature works. Instant reward-systems are definitely great for getting the young to do what you want them to do. Children do the work asked of them, which makes the adult happy, and the young-one gets the reward, which makes the child happy. It is a system based on the immediate need for results and is an absolute fabrication. Within the actual nature of life, abundance is consistently overflowing, and to obtain a certain goal we sometimes will work and work with no obvious improvement in sight. No immediate feedback. Our sight sensory function may not feedback to the brain what is understood as a successful action as an instant gratification was not met. The brain believes nothing is occurring as it cannot see anything occurring and the consciousness may choose to halt the action. Yet the *progress* of the seed sits *under* the ground and the workings to the sight function is not visible. Instead we see dirt, this and nothing more. Should we then halt the action of cultivation at this point, we would also halt the unseen progress occurring just beneath the surface.

Life is a constant and consistent source of abundance and delusions have integrated into our society to where we now believe if we have no money we have nothing. We have forgotten the whispers of the angels. Money is the chosen and created currency of the western world where in other cultures it may be a cow or food or gestures. It is an idea and nothing more. Money, as the crops of the great farmer can be cultivated using the currency that is everlasting, supplied to us by the ever-existing. Currency is just something of value that we trade for something else of value and there is nothing of greater value on this planet than the power of the human mind.

I repeat; the master-skill is to cultivate regardless. There are things happening beyond our five senses that are continually responding to your cultivations, bringing them to fruition. Cultivate regardless, the thing that you most desire, regardless of pain, regardless of perceived failure, regardless of the nay-sayers and experts advising you away from your goal and you will harvest what it is that you have nurtured. This is the nature of success and progress. The master-skill.

Reading this and knowing this is pointless. Feeling inspired is hopeless. Space is necessary to meditate on our true nature and value. It must be supremely understood and not simply "known". It must be weaved into, fully saturated and allowed to permeate deep into the very core of our being and not simply "inspired".

Knowing can happen in a day and can make us feel fantastic for a moment or three, yet to become fully understanding to the laws that govern our trajectory and to walk the line every day, as mentioned above, requires a full saturation, an immersion into, a full and deliberate re-programming of the sub-conscious programming (if it is not serving your conscious wishes). This is the only way you can transform from non-belief to knowing to understanding and finally to believing. Once belief is the founding factor of your goals and aims, everything else gets in line. The subconscious will then understand your new choice as *fact* and will conspire to bring it all to a full manifestation. This is the point and this is the key. Now you know. It *still* means nothing and will do you no good until you believe it will with all of your being.

Begin to fabricate a new world around you whether it is already there or not. Read and be inspired in every single moment. Listen to the great speakers who find no excuse in failure or solace in blame and read books by authors of the same. Create a list of inspiration to listen to and learn from. Continually leave yourself open to inspiration. Listen to the natural wisdom in the breeze and in the silence and maintain awareness of your states of emotion. Maintain and maintain some more the greatness that life has to offer within your own existence. If it does not come your way then go and find it. Yearn for experience and settle not for the mundane for it was not your nature at your dawn nor should it be considered so when comes your dusk.

Knowing and inspiration are like short fuses to a bomb that emits an uneventful and counter-productive pop. Begin to understand and conspire to formulate a life that *becomes* pure belief. The responsibility is always, and always ever will be, your own. Upon doing this, you will, with all the burning an all-consuming desire can bring, work to achieve your goal or die trying, yet, if you should die before achieving the goal you will not go to the grave with regret and futility. You would have died fighting for what you believe in and that is truly inspiring. That is the strength and the resolve that becomes necessary when obtaining a life of your design. That is the warrior's way. Seek and be inspired. Create a desire that is a raging inferno that razes obstacles in your path. Be wise. Be compassionate and be vigilant.

Part Two

Kaden's Fable

"MANY, MANY YEARS AGO IN a sad, faraway land, there was an enormous mountain made of rough, black stone. At sunset, on top of that mountain, a magic rose blossomed every night that made whoever plucked it immortal. But no one ever dared go near it because its thorns were full of poison. Men talked among themselves about their fear of death and pain but never about the promise of eternal life. And every day, the rose wilted, unable to bequeath its gift to anyone... forgotten and lost atop that cold, dark mountain, forever alone, until the end of time."

"El Laberinto del Fauno" (later promoted as "Pan's Labyrinth")

Not only is this a very beautiful piece of writing, it also illustrates the focus many people take when there is a prize to be sought. The fact that the rose held the prize of immortality that men so desired was the only cause for them to speak of its thorns and the fate that lay within them. However, in speaking of the horror of the thorns they completely neglected the magic that the rose could bequeath. The mountain of rough, black stone illustrates the struggle that lay before the prize and the sunset illustrates each new day's opportunity to seek our bravery and to be aware of life's opportunities. All of these things go hand in hand. They are partnered together. In order to gain the prize the folly would be to *focus* on the danger. What would prove more beneficial would be to recognise and prepare for the long and arduous climb, the struggle, with the thought of the goal in mind. To understand that the danger of the thorns exist but that with patience, preparation and careful execution, the prize can definitely be obtained. It is not the same if someone does all the work, climbs the mountain, risks the failure gains the prize only to hand to you the rose. The gift has already been claimed and what is being handed to you is empty. The struggle, the pain and the pleasure are all part of the same package. Within the journey to obtain the life of your design, if you are not prepared to fight through the hard times, than you simply have not earned the good times.

FOUR MEN SAT TOGETHER DISCUSSING, over an ale, the legend of the rose. Two of the men, Melchiah and Titus, were convinced by the third, Kaden, to make the climb that would see them pluck the magic rose from the top of that black and looming mountain. The forth man, Dumah, wanting nothing to do with the discussion and thinking Kaden insane for even suggesting such a thing, picked himself up and left but not before leaving a piece of his mind; "Kaden you are a great fool and if the two of you take his fool-ness upon yourselves then you are both even greater fools! Atop that mount you will find nothing but your deaths. Each of you. This is my advice to you, take heed or see yourselves die as a party of fools." As Dumah left Kaden explained to the two remaining that he had devised a plan, he told them that he *knew* beyond a shadow of a doubt that the rose *existed* atop that black mountain and that he *believed completely* in its promise for immortality. Furthermore; he had created a plan regarding the mountain and its climb, the dangers he predicted and how to approach and counter them. The pitfalls and how he had intended to avoid them. The terrain and the weather and how to prepare for them. Once at the top, he had a plan, which he believed would work, on how to pluck the rose safely from its root without injury and thus, gaining its promise for immortality. He assured the others that he knew his plan *would* work and that, if they followed him all the way and were to make the dangerous climb with him, then they can have the secret plans for themselves. With reluctance, they agreed to partner the mission.

They met within a few days, at sunset, at the foot of the mountain and gazed up at its summit for a long while... "This is suicide..." Melchiah thought aloud as he looked upon the steep, sheerness of the dark, black rock gracing the monolith before them. "There is *no way* you can be *sure* there is even a rose up there. And *if* you were to survive the climb to discover a rose, there is no certainty in its legend. This is *madness for sure.*" Kaden responded: "I *am* sure beyond a doubt. I see it at every moment in my mind's eye. I don't know *how* but I know that it *is* up there and I know that it will be in my possession. All I need do is to begin the climb, start the journey and by the end I *will* have achieved what I have said I will. However, I cannot explain further. The choice is yours but if you are to go then be-gone now for your negativity infects my focus." Overcome with doubt Melchiah made a haste departure but not before he too, like Dumah before him, left a piece of his mind: "My friends I am concerned, please take my advice from a caring heart that this mission will be your pointless suicide should you continue. Go home now. Turn back and forget this foolish dream!" Now there were only the two. Kaden turned to Titus, "... And what of you? Do you trust my vision or will you too follow doubt?" Titus explained: "I am not as sure as you are Kaden, however I believe that *you* believe what you say. I know you not to be a man of rash decision and, even if there is a chance that you are right, I choose to follow you for the reward far outweighs the lifetime of doubt if I do not." Thus the two men began the climb.

Here we have an illustration of the importance of the vision. Kaden said that he saw in his mind's eye the success that he would achieve and he saw it vividly at every point that he could. The fact that I came to find is that the brain does not have the ability to decipher what is real from what is unreal. So when you visualise, when you see yourself performing the actions that you desire over and over again, when you can feel it in your heart, your brain begins to *believe* that this is reality. Belief exists in the conscious mind and whatever is impressed upon the conscious mind consistently and over a long period of time, begins to be recognised as fact within the subconscious mind. A fact in the subconscious mind is defended and begins to be actualised and actioned throughout the body. That is to say that the subconscious mind will actually take what is belief and begin, with constant diligence, to manifest it within the real world. Having a vision is key to achieving the goal and the key to vision is belief in the goal.

In the beginning of the story there were four men. The third, Kaden, is the man with the vision of success. The other three men represent the attitudes that you will face from others (and yourself) once you are convinced that your dream is your reality and that you will not stop until you have it manifested in your life.

Benjamin Fairbairn

Dumah; the Scoffer

IN DUMAH WE FIND THE *scoffer*. He is the *protector* of the norm and the defender of the status quo. His bane is that of a deeply woven and unrelenting *fear* of *progression*. For him, to venture forth into the unknown brings only the possibility of destruction and even the notion of adventure with abandonment is considered a fool's venture. The life he protects is *by far* the life that he desires, his desires come to him in the form of *envy*. However, he protects this due to a fear of losing whatever little he has. His artillery is the *skilful* use of *ridicule* which is fired *mercilessly* and without lack at any sign of a dream chaser. His armour is that of pillowed *comfort* and is the protection he uses from any who would *dare* to lacerate him with the suggestion of another throw at his destiny. He has built *complacency* as his *fortress*, where from, within the thick and heavy walls, he finds refuge and protection and, to which, only *he* holds the key. To try and convince the scoffer is the greatest errand a fool can take no matter his guise, which can be that of associates, friends and even the beloved family. To combat, remove him from your sight. Deafen yourself from his *slander* and save your precious speech from him as his language is *archaic* and his energy holds the *potency* of infective *negativity*. Each word spoken in his direction is as hopeless as the limb-less child mired in quicksand. Cruelty may not be the intention of the scoffer and they may mean no harm, however, they are *extremely* harmful if *you* allow them to be. They can be aggressive or passive, however they will *always* show up to bring you down, sometimes without even knowing that they do so. They are sitting comfortably in their discontent and are ready to shoot down any who they choose whilst seated in their throne of garbage.

Benjamin Fairbairn

Melchiah; the Concerned Friend

THE SECOND MAN TOO LEAVE is the friend with kindly advice, in this case: Melchiah. This well-wisher believed in your idea and your dream when it was a story over a pint or an adventure to have fun with. But when it became all too real, he lacked the *vision* and the *courage* necessary to continue. This is all well and good, as every man must take his own journey in his own time, however, not content in stepping aside for his own good, this friend will try to "advise" you away from your goal. He comes from a place of genuine care and truly has your best interests at heart. But his best interests stem from a place of *fear* and *protection*. A fear of failure and a protection against the disturbance within the way things are. You are his *friend* and what you are attempting has every potential to change your course and *connection* with him, in one way or another, forever. With *ignorance* he tells you fervently of his opinion and of your foolhardiness if you decide against his advice. He will become animated with energy as he throws logic and reason before you in an attempt to stray you from your mad and foolish thoughts. He does not understand your vision, yet he understands that your journey *will* separate you from past accomplices if they are not *beneficial* to your aim. This is a natural separation and the caring and fearful friend knows this within his heart. He wants his pal to sit with him for he has much more to say, mired in a beer-stained velour seat, mulling over good times once gone distracting you from good times yet-to-come. This man has been there for you in past times to spill tears and alcohol when it was needed but *now* is the time for

93

more. Now is the time to stand tall for what you know will be done. Let your friend know that he is appreciated and that you are *not ignorant* and explain no more. His final attempts will be to insult you, however you must be aware that, to the fool *you* are the fool. Wish him well and move forward in your quest. Never once looking back.

Fear, Doubt and Anxiety

The icy rock radiated pain back onto the blushed and numbed faces of the climbers. The sleek surface offered an almost grip-less challenge that had been thence-forth untested by any man. The winds swept across in an onslaught that threatened to carry them to their deaths or to freeze them where they scaled. This was Kaden's mission that had penetrated every wakened and slumbered moment for the last three months. During the days previous, onlookers would see his physicality sitting while, through his eyes, they could discern that he was clearly elsewhere. He had conquered this mountain one million times within his mind. He had plucked the rose and gained from it the contained promise. Then he began again at the foot of the mountain to commence the climb, stone by stone once again. His belief had convinced but one to follow him; Titus. However as they ascended higher, as each hand, frozen into clawed position, clambered for juts to heave tired dead-weight skyward up the precipice and as the ground beneath them misted into memory, the trust and belief that Titus held began to wane. He had not the strength to shout to Kaden and the Earth's screaming breath that surged upon them was far too loud and would thus carry his protest into obscurity. The power it would take to do this, he had decided, was best reserved to the matter at hand. Soon through the painful upheaval they reached a footing which led to an opening within the escarpment. Here it was that they decided to rest and rejuvenate before they continued the journey. They had not climbed, as yet, four-thousand meters...

... "Kaden... Kaden!" Titus used this opportunity to heft a scream as to break the frost from his lungs and to gain his companions attention. "Tell me, what of now? How holds your reserve? Do you still believe in making it to the summit or have you a plan for our descent *back* to our homes? It is not yet too late to turn back!" As the question echoed through the cave it had no effect on Kaden's ears. "Kaden I say! What of our descent?!" "Our descent..." Snapped Kaden's interruption, "... comes with rose in hand and not before... What did you think this would feel like Titus? What part of my plan involved God's angels carrying us to the summit with ease within the warmed beam of heaven's gaze?"

Titus stood unknowing of what to say yet could only plead further. "My friend, this *is* madness as warned by Melchiah. My body is racked with pain as is my mind at the thought of leaving this mouth to the fierce and unforgiving whims of that cruel cold." Titus pointed to the violent storm. "I fear this task. I fear it from marrow to ether. Please... I beg of you to see sense."

"I see only one thing my friend. I see our winning this mountain as I have seen a million times before. I have calculated everything including the pain that reverberates within us *both*! There can be no *prize* without *pain* Titus. I explained this to you with clarity and *you* made your *choice*! I will explain no further and leave you to your decision hence-forth with no contest... Do as you please... You know the fastest method of descent from here...

...Feel free to take it."

Seeing his friend's determination as hubris, Titus, hungry, freezing, tired and confused could only look outwards to blame and rage to keep him warm. "...If we should die up here, be it on your head Kaden! ...You who widowed my wife and left my children father-less!
You who shattered my family!"
Kaden walked deeper into the cave and slumped heavily to a sit, removing food from his satchel he returned voice calmly to Titus: "Whatever thoughts allow you peace my brother. I know my goal and I have faith in it. I applied no violent coerce when you accepted my offer. You did so freely."
Despite his apparent confidence, Kaden was weary from this first climb and his chest was heavy laden. The first seedlings of doubt had sown in and the coming precipitation of pain had begun to nurture this doubt. The clothing he wore to protect him from the cold had almost frozen solid which made horizontal movement laborious and vertical seem almost impossible. His fingers had become large, swollen and extremely painful. He understood the doubt of all and yet, through his own pain and his own doubt, his hope and vision were the only things that fought back the fear, the frustration and the pain that were all growing stronger as every minute dwindled by. He had his plan and he *would* see it through to the end.

How could Kaden possibly know what he claimed to know? How could he be so sure in the face of so much doubt? He had nothing he could use to prove his determination at the point of saying so and how could he keep his determination in the face of such opposition? Opposition that also, deep within his own belief, made some semblance of sense...

Benjamin Fairbairn

The Close and Precious Friend

THERE WILL ALWAYS BE PEOPLE who will try to deny us our success whether it be the scoffer or the genuinely concerned and "well-informed" friend and these people, with no malice, can be ignored and turned away from. They are entitled to their opinion and it is up to us as to whether we stand and allow our vision to be shot down or whether to hear the echoes of the gunshot preceding and to choose avoid the red-zone altogether. Choose wisely and those sounds will become so far in the distance you will hardly ever hear them again. That is not to say that healthy opposition is to be altogether avoided but, until you have gained a worthy case to defend, there is no point in standing by whilst having your dreams gunned down in front of you. We ought to be allowed to try and to fail. It is exactly through this process that we learn and we grow. But what if the opposition to your goal is, as is very often and most commonly the case, a close and precious loved one? Our spouse or parent? Brother or sister? What if we cannot altogether walk away from this opposition? It is important to realise that their ideas may be coming from a place of genuine concern and there is no doubt over their best interests. However, they have not shared your dreams. They have not mustered the desire that you have and allowed their thoughts to become overwhelmed with visions of the desire in question thus they will never understand your belief nor is it likely that you will be able to infuse the same belief within them. All that can be said of this moment and those in fear of your goal failing for you is this: *they will either unveil your lack of belief within your dream or they will aid in galvanising it.*

It was little less than half-way to the summit before Titus was lost. Was it his doubts that had finally overcome his ability to persevere? He experienced his final moments plunging backward in fear and disbelief toward the ground he so longed for. His eyes fixated on Kaden's own as he felt the g-force augment him internally and then he was no more. Witnessing his companion disappear from sight, there was nothing else that Kaden could do but to continue on climbing toward the goal. Without a doubt, safe descent was now far simpler via a route from the top then from where he now clung. Now was not the time to mourn for Titus, his dear friend. He needed every ounce of reserve that he could muster for the climb through the icy blades of wind. No time to ponder on their last moments together. No time for regret nor words that might have been spoken or deeds done. Should he stop to mourn he would most surely perish upon this mountain for the effects of misery would permeate into his belief to the point where he too would eventually meet just as grisly an end.

Kaden knew the reason Titus had lost his grip upon the mountain was because he willed it unwittingly. He saw death, he envisioned the fall and his demise. He feared it with every fibre of his being, fortifying his emotion to this end. Thus, his emotional artillery was not focused on survival but failure. Kaden believed in the deepest chasms of his being that the fate of Titus would not befall himself as he had faith that his aim would fall true. With each painful and slow upheaval of his burdensome frame, housed in frozen and cumbersome clothing, satchels hanging pendulous, threatening to entangle his limbs mischievously, and send him plummeting, his moments of doubts and fears had passed. Each muscle painfully burned, yet he fed upon it. His ligaments were akin to the effects of rigor mortis, on the brink of snapping sharply with every strain. Yet he fought upward against the mighty gravitational pull imbued with the drag of the fierce and unrelenting weather.

As he made the summit there were no celebrations. Not yet. Now was not the time. Worn and beaten down, Kaden crawled and rolled to a safe crevice where he instinctively knew that he could safely pass into unconsciousness... And so he did.

When we look back at Kaden's journey there was not a moment where he forced any of the men to do a single thing that was against their own better judgement. He had an idea, a dream, a desire and a plan. Kaden's major mistake was to share his views with those who had no business in knowing.

"Cast not your pearls before the swine, lest they trample them, then turn and rend you".

Matthew Chapter: 7. Verse: 6. The Bible

Benjamin Fairbairn

Dreams and Ideas

HAVING A DREAM AND AN IDEA has never been an amazing achievement throughout the span of human history. All of us at some point have had big dreams and big ideas. Walking through the cemetery one summer afternoon brought to me a thought as I became overwhelmed by the silence and peace there. I looked and was drawn to one stone in particular that was covered in moss and had been burped sideways by an aged earth. I walked up to it and rubbed some of the green away. The stone noted a man that was buried in 1861. He had left behind a wife and a child and they had been married for four years. I began to day-dream about this man and his wife. A couple who were strangers and became lovers. I dreamed about the emotions each must have felt when they first saw each other and the trials they may have had to go through in order to meet for their very first date. On the date they smiled at each other and drew close. Their hearts would beat faster almost uncomfortably as they saw their futures in each other's eyes. At that moment the world and its fore-coming was full of hope and dreams and possibilities. He promised her that he would bring her the world and that he would make it his life's work to do her proud. I dreamed about his happiness when she said they were having a baby and his concern when she was giving birth. Of them holding the child in their arms and watching as the process of life began again in her. I felt the energy that surrounded them as they lived their lives together; powerful and real. I saw their problems and trials which caused them to say hurtful things to each other. The awkwardness as he came to say that he was sorry. I saw the events of their life unfurl inside my mind and then I opened my eyes to see once again the stone. All that was left of the hopes and dreams lost forever in space and time with no one left to even visit and take care of a stone. I was overwhelmed with sadness as this stone spoke to me. I realised the lives that meant so much, the energy that worked so hard to keep this body, this love and dreams alive was now nothing but forgotten, then I turned, I saw hundreds more. All souls that had hopes and dreams and loves and goals and tragedies. Hundreds. All that remained of their dreams and goals now were stones, cracked, worn and forgotten. How many had their dreams fulfilled and how many waited for a day that never came?

No. Having the dream or the idea to do something is never the difficult part. The soil is fortified with those who had dreams and ideas. The true issue comes in three parts.

Part One: Ridicule and the Lack of Belief

THE FIRST BEING THAT OF having an idea that is against common acceptance. The reason I say this is because having an idea to do well and to provide is not a dream, it is a human necessity. We dream because we have no opportunity to touch and feel and experience our dreams until it is real. Perhaps your idea seems foolish or ridiculous to others. This is due to many reasons. Perhaps they once had the same idea and it didn't work out for them thus, *in their experience,* the idea is destined to fail and its pursuit is a foolish one? It could also be that they believe the idea is too difficult and that you would be dunderheaded to even attempt such a feat? It *is* also possible that they are jealous with your vigour and see something in you that they wish they had but are aimless as of how to attain it. It may even be that your idea is to be a mother with a man that others do not approve of. An identity that you feel compelled to embrace that others do not understand. Whatever the reasons may be for their disdain towards your idea or compulsion you would do well to understand that it is not your concern as to what they think. They are coming from a place that is laden with a plethoric history of experiences that have nothing to do with you, so to seek acceptance from them is less of a necessity than it seems. We must ask ourselves why we have convinced ourselves of its importance. It is never easy going against the grain and when faced with opposition of any kind, as Kaden also experienced, many flounder under the pressure of fear, rejection and ridicule. Their vision hasn't the power to overcome the immediate ridicule and scorn of those who don't understand and they part ways with their dreams, their desires and their goals to regain the common acceptance that they risked losing. They pull themselves from the line of fire taking the quickest route they know. They get back on the train to mediocrity and regret whilst watching destination: opportunity disappear into the distance.

Part Two: Positive Association and Doing the Work

THE SECOND PART OF THE issue was in the company of which Kaden chose to confide. Namely; anybody. In this and most commonly every single case, before we learn any better, should we come upon a great idea, we tend to tell those closest to us; family, friends, lovers, associates and sometimes even random strangers we've known for nigh moments. This is a completely natural compulsion that comes from the need to appear worthy to our peers and must be eradicated at all costs. It is a sign that we are unsure of our own worth; a lacking in the belief of the esteem we hold for ourselves. We are all potent with power and miracles occurring within us at every moment. Believe this and convince only yourself of your vision and you will not fall victim to the second part of the issue. This is very important. When a good and close friend saw the flecks of promotion I had perpetuated regarding my company she congratulated me and said that I did it so quickly. She said that others take an awful long time to get a business off the ground and that mine had just seemed to pop up out of nowhere. Of course she didn't know that I had laboured over two years of trials and errors and endless days and nights of arduous study. She didn't know because I told no one who didn't need to know. I sought guidance from those who could help and I followed the laws of acquisition. All people ever see are the results and if it is done very well it appears to have come all too easily. Seek the advice of those who really know, anything other than this is just blowing smoke. There is nothing in the conjuring of a good idea, it means absolutely nothing until the work is done. *The proof is in the pudding!* There is a saying that; the word "water" cannot quench your thirst for it is just a word. It is only the substance that will ever sate you.

Anybody growing up on this planet would have come to realise by now that absolutely everybody is an expert and everybody has an expert opinion if you ask them for it and that is what most people do. Kaden told his buddies about his dream and his vision and he received mixed reactions and none of them were positive. Advice, like anything, is a double edged sword and can bring either fortunate results or the latter, it is simply a matter of asking the advice of the right people. The right people are *not* your favourite people. They may not be the Father you are trying to impress, the girl you are trying to sway or the circle of friends whose approval you seek. And they may not be the ones who merely talk like they know how. The advice you seek must come from those who have been and experienced it and achieved success. The success of each heave-ho up the mountain to your goal depends on the choices you make. Seek your advisers with great care.

Understand fully the intentions that you have created for your life and let none infect doubt upon you, yet stay aware of the good experience in people that can really prove to benefit your goal. Help those of whom you can provide good use yet never do so unwittingly. Once you have grown fully aware of your intentions never again allow precious time to be idly swept away from under you.

Part Three: Discipline

THE THIRD IS IN THE discipline that is needed to take the necessary actions in order to strive for what you tell yourself that you want.

Simple as it may sound, the greatest divergence to your goals of which you must be aware of, the sneakiest of snakes to your intentions that you must set traps for is and will always be your-very-own-sweet-self.

'Set your sights upon the heights, don't be a mediocrity.
Don't just wait and trust in fate and say:
"that's how it's meant to be"
It's up to you how far you go.
If you don't try you'll never know!
And so my lad, as I've explained,
nothing ventured nothing gained!
Aba do da de dum. Ba de da bo...'
Merlin – The sword in the Stone

Benjamin Fairbairn

The Power of People

JUST AS PEOPLE HAVE THE *potential* to affect your downfall, should *you* allow them to, there are also those who hold the potential to have just as vibrant an effect upon your life ... *should* you allow them to. In today's world it can be easy to become carried away with the tide of misery and woe that constantly collides against us and we may find ourselves thinking "why should I even try? What's the point?" It can be a strain to believe that there can be good, productive and positive people in the world today achieving very highly at what they choose whilst helping to make lives better for others along the way. It is difficult to feel that, whatsoever we should want to achieve in this life there will always be people to support us in our endeavours and, not only support, but to advise us adequately and accurately as to a path that may bide us well. It is true that finding these people is far more challenging than finding those who are ready to throw your dreams to the pre-dug grave, such is life. However the good people are there and they are in absolute abundance, should we actually *want* to find them. These people will know what we need to do to attain our wishes and can guide us to the roads we need to journey. However they cannot take the journey for us and most of the advice we will receive will be honest and not all to our liking as it will mean some hard-time and hard-work in a beneficial direction. This is exactly what Kaden found out about in his journey. He may have gained advice from experienced mountaineers yet no one could bear the climb for him regardless of how sound their advice and information may have been.

Understanding this has been an invaluable achievement for myself as, as I have mentioned earlier, I once abhorred the human race with every ounce of my being and believed that every single person, given the opportunity, would welcome with open arms the most foulest of every human trait imaginable, therefore I would have welcomed upon them the very same. I have witnessed and experienced enough to now know different. Of course if we paint our walls black then black is all we will see. Advice is ours to take or leave; as is the journey to our goals. What I *have* discovered through my experience is this: if we are open to kindness then we will find kindness opens to us and if we will administer kindness we will not have to wait long before kindness is administered back to us. It's good to know that the reason people react to us in a certain way is mostly our own responsibility. That puts the power right back into our own hands.

When I was a child there were two brothers, Ricky and Jimmy, who were similar in age to me, who lived a few doors down and with whom we used to (my sisters and I) meet up and play with often. We knew them quite well and so one day, as I was walking back home from buying my father's newspaper, which now stayed closed all the way home, I noticed one of the boys, Jimmy – the older brother, outside his house. He was doing something with his bike and, as I passed by, I waved and said "hello". He glanced at me and completely, totally and absolutely ignored my hello and continued working on his bike. I remember feeling terribly embarrassed and foolish also became very angry and made the vow there and then to *never-ever* greet anybody first ever again. Even if I knew them, if they wanted to talk they would have to come to *me* first. I was still young enough for this experience to shoot straight through into my subconscious programming and set a standard that I would protect vigilantly. I became a stand-offish rudeling. I never made friends thereon. If I had any friends it was *them* who made *me*. That little, insignificant moment had such an impact on that little boy that he never ever made the first move again. The defence against his fear of rejection had been set and he would never deviate for fear of that rejection being relived. No one was around to see the last one and as I grew older the justification of fear grew within me. I became a reactionary-being not doing anything unless first initiated by another as now I was older and if I was to get rejected in the same or similar manner and should anyone see it this time, I believed that my world would implode!

Benjamin Fairbairn

The Complexities of Mankind

SOCIETY MAY BE A STRANGE and tragic beast but the same cannot generally be said for the people within it for the simple reason that the stars in our galaxy were mapped out long before the unravelling of the complexities of man were ever even attempted. We've always been observed by each other ever since the dawn of the crudest method of recording was first utilised and many ideas were thrown into the simmering pot by philosophers, poets and theologians of every ilk. Yet these have always been ideas, opinions and musings. Man split the atom and explored embryonic life long before actively exploring how or why we operate as humans became feasible as a possibility. It cannot yet be said with any definiteness that man is good or evil in nature as good and evil will always be subjective in its *own* nature. What I do know is that the more I invest in people with a drive greater than mine, abilities more skilled than my own and compassion deeper than I possess, I become inspired and imbued by them as opposed to those of when I was a darkling, writhing in the shadows; beastly and angry. I didn't seek those greater than I, I sought those agreeable to my famished thoughts who would plume me with agreeable responses. People to relate to my agony. People who felt the same. Head-nodders of yes. I sought confirmation for my thoughts rather than challenge which meant, although I was mired in a dark, deep hole, I wasn't alone. I found people who could suffer like me and with me. None of us able to pull free, content to dwell in the rolling echoes of our own suffering.

Benjamin Fairbairn

It's Not You, It's Me

HAVE YOU EVER WONDERED WHY you have the friends that you do or how we end up in the relationships that we find ourselves in? Have you ever looked at your partner and been stumped as to how you ever got together in the first place? Could it be because at some point in your lives you were both on the same vibratory frequency and you're not on the same frequency any longer?

Everything on this planet appears as it does due to its vibratory frequency. As mentioned earlier in the section "Altered states", water is vibrating at a corporeal state, in the sense that it can be experienced with the five sense funnels. We found that if the water is heated to a certain temperature it is no longer in a corporeal vibration, it is now in an astral vibration that we can call steam and if we continue to heat it up it will change its vibratory state again and move up a frequency to the state of air and so forth. This is called the water-cycle and we all know this. However we only know this because that is what we have been taught, so it exists in our intellect as *reason* as it makes *sense* to us.

As we all know this occurs within the water-cycle, is it then so challenging to comprehend that our states of change are also of a vibratory nature and that the energy we put out attracts an energy that is vibrating at the same frequency, right back to us?

With this in mind, would it not then be righteous to be aware of our own vibratory frequency when gaining buddies and chums? At an aggressive rate you will attract only other aggressors. Thus is it not far more important to be aware of our own vibratory frequency and where we ourselves are currently sitting on the spectrum than it is to know anything regarding the others? Our company and life are perfect indicators of where we are on the spectrum at any given moment. If we were not satisfied with the company we keep, our partners or the reactions and responses we experience from the outside world, would it not make sense then, to change this by altering our own vibratory frequency? In short, if you seem to be attracting the wrong sort than you can be sure that you are representing that sort within your own actions literally calling them unto you with your own energy.

A hard pill to swallow, but then responsibility always is. The people in our lives are there only because we invited them to be there. We are the guards to and masters of our own experience. Thus it goes to say that, if we want more interesting people in our lives, then we had better become more interesting ourselves and the best place to start with here is to become more *interested!*

I have, of the people in this world, of whom I once considered to be disgusting wastes of flesh breathing my air, since adopted the understanding, not through preference nor trend, but through emancipating experience, that we – the people, are not only miraculous creatures by definition but are also one of the most compelling and incredible forms of creation this planet has to offer with the *tendency* to help, love and struggle for the good of others. I do however, italicize the word *"tendency"* in order to elaborate it as such. Science Professor and author James Harvey Robinson had this to say in 1921: *"Suspicion and hate are much more congenial to our natures than love, for very obvious reasons in this world of rivalry and common failure. There is, beyond a doubt, a natural kindliness in mankind that will show itself under favourable auspices."* Rod Serling masterfully spoke on this in his episode of The Twilight Zone: *" **The Monsters Are Due on Maple Street***": *"The tools of conquest do not necessarily come with bombs and explosions and fallout.*

There are weapons that are simply thoughts, attitudes, prejudices – to be found only in the minds of men. For the record, prejudices can kill, suspicion can destroy and a thoughtless frightened search for a scapegoat has a fallout all of its own for the children and the children yet unborn. And the pity is that these things cannot be confined – to the Twilight Zone."

As man, by its nature, is a survivor, this thread of suspicion, fear of wrong doing towards oneself and the hate of something that may be perceived as harmful or disrupting to the way things are can lead to prejudices and even the deaths of our fellow man. However, as mentioned above by James Harvey Robinson; in favourable circumstances, which we may be fortunate enough to live in today, most people are of favourable countenance and can be sought and gathered by becoming more favourable within ourselves and within our own actions.

Benjamin Fairbairn

The Dawn of Great Opportunity

TODAY WE ARE (REGARDLESS OF whatever hole we may have dug ourselves in or have chosen to dig ourselves deeper into) sugared with opportunity like never before in the history of mankind, and we would do well to remember that the greatest of our ilk found their way to their own opportunity in the grittiest and most sordid of environments and circumstances. There was not the grace of educational courses, many of which can be found for no cost whatsoever, as which to better our "unfortunate" circumstance. There was not the miracle of an information highway with the ability to say what we want to millions of people all at the same time at the touch of a button like we have today. In 2017; a six year old child was estimated to be worth approximately eight-million pounds after his parents opened a channel of him reviewing toys on YouTube and was, of course, unaware of the fact that he was earning anything at all. There was not the freedom of speech and identity that we have today that allows us to live and say as we please. Of course there will always be racists, homophobes and anti-everythings as there always has been. We can never infiltrate every heart on the planet, yet we always have the opportunity to work on our own. Their hate is mostly no longer bound to or enforced by any law. Something which we could not always proclaim.

Today there are men and women earning millions teaching the masses how to walk and how to talk. How to dress and how to undress. How to eat and how to breathe. Earning money has never been an issue as there has always been men and women who earn lots of money. Regardless of those who would blame dark beginnings, bad times and a lack of chances to find success, it was never a question of any of these tiresome excuses but a question of our emotional connection to the excuses partnered with our reactions to them. Be aware that the success you wish for, the success you fear and the success that you believe you do not deserve are one in the same if you have not yet convinced yourself otherwise.

We are made up by a complex myriad of waves and notions and what we ever only see of anyone is one side of the very tip of a vast and deep pyramid. However if we would ever want to know something of what lies beneath the surface we have only to look as far as ourselves. There is nothing we could want to find in someone that we cannot first find in the mirror as we are the reflection of every other thing in this world as far as we have seen it. We are as similar to the ocean as it is similar to itself. We only ever need to look within to see the world and to understand its inhabitants. If you cannot stand people you can be sure that there is something that you cannot stand within yourself. However, unravelling the onion that is our mind will without a doubt reveal pungent layers sure to bring tears to our eyes. It is our innate impulse to defend everything that we think is us. Take as an example a couple on a date; the man has complimented the lady: "you have the most wonderful, beautiful eyes." The lady, blushed, unknowing how to react to the compliment responds with a rebuff: "Oh, they are puffy and tired. They're so ugly." Humans are mostly at comfort when insulting themselves. The man, enlightened to the puffy redness of her tired eyes stands corrected; "Ah yes, I see what you mean! Horrid are your bulbous orbs!" The woman, shocked, pours a beverage over the man's head and walks away, insulted and infuriated. How dare he agree with her?! We are attuned to defend what is ours in one way or another, whether we know why we do it or not. It is not difficult to understand that wars have razed homes and lives to the ground all in the name of defence of a particular belief that another had offended.

Beings have been treated severely simply for proclaiming a belief that is in contradiction to a widely accepted other. Like philosopher and Dominican friar Giordano Bruno who was burned alive for stating that the Earth revolved around the sun in a period when the widely accepted truth was the opposite.

"Truth does not change because it is, or is not, believed by a majority of the people."

Giordano Bruno

In order to truly be free to accept the possibility that we are supported in this world it all begins in how we see it. Not from defending a limiting thought that we have paid no mind as to how it appeared there in the first place or by assuming that the world is a grand utopia and that there is nay an unfortunate thing nor person upon it. The fact is that there is only one world and that is the one that we, each as individuals, choose it to be. Paradoxically there are millions of worlds and realities. Your world and its inhabitants can either support your journey or it and they can provide you with a dead-end at every turn you take. The choice is, as it has always been, y-ours.

Benjamin Fairbairn

On Diligence

Benjamin Fairbairn

The Great Cornelius

PSYCHOLOGISTS USED TO BELIEVE THAT we had one aspect to the mind and that aspect was our conscious mind or "the awake mind". Within this we would be able to think, choose, originate, reason and imagine. Your conscious mind held your will and it was the thing that operated to get us through from day to day. If your choices of behaviour were not civilised or were of a confusing nature, lobotomies and a life-time of medication within the walls of a mental-facility were things of the norm. For some cases of anxiety (something that is prolific within current times) the fibres of the brain in the vicinity of the thalamus was sliced up in order to reduce the anxiety. Today however, we know better. Call it what you will, you will notice that there is something deeper than the daily thoughts brought forth by our consciousness. Some call it the abdominal mind or the "being" mind. Others may call it the unconscious, the subconscious mind or the sleeping mind. Doctor Joseph Murphy, in his book: *"The Power of the Subconscious Mind"*, pronounced that it is the thing we are talking to when we pray (and he was a minister). Some people may call it: *the universe*, the point is, whatever you may choose to call it, there is something within the depths of the mind that was awake *before* the awakening of consciousness. For the sake of the narrative we will refer to it as: Cornelius.

Benjamin Fairbairn

The Five Sense Funnels

WHEN WE WERE BABIES CORNELIUS was open wide and ready to be filled with all that the world had to offer. There were five sense funnels which allowed everything around Cornelius to be guided directly into it and as there were no filters on the funnels there was no discriminations as to what went in. There were no boundaries and all was fair game. Everything flowed in freely. The five sense funnels are as follows:

1. **The sight funnel**: Every kaleidoscopic vision that surrounded the child was sucked into the sight funnel as light into a black-hole and became one with Cornelius.

2. **The scent funnel**: An assault of smells; both pungent and sweet funnelled into Cornelius.

3. **The sound funnel**: Cries of joy and pain, laughter and sorrow, whispered and screamed burrowed deep into Cornelius' depths via the sound funnel.

4. **The taste funnel**: Bitter and sweetness, some a pleasure and some not so. All variations were fed to the taste funnel.

5. **The touch funnel**: Sensations electrify, caress and tear their way through the touch funnel.

Everything merged into Cornelius, forming experience and never once did it ask for confirmation as to what anything was, nothing had to pass any tests nor were held back due to prejudices or preferences. Everything that went into Cornelius went in freely, filling it to the brim with experience and with each new addition a **filter** was being formed. As the child reached adolescence the filter was complete and it was named: *Consciousness*. Cornelius was now more powerful than ever; unstoppable and uncompromising. Cornelius piloted the consciousness via the human vessel for it had gathered all the data it needed in order to begin its journey towards the intended destination. Cornelius would be damned if it would allow anything to get in its way or to hinder the mission at hand.

Cornelius was now in full control and held an enormous power that had been built by its environment and the whisperings of its inhabitants and now, unawares to the child vessel, it had its identity and destiny fortified.

We all have a Cornelius that lives below our consciousness which is essentially our guidance system and it is filled with our prejudices, our beliefs, expectations and the images we hold of ourselves. Who we believe ourselves to be and what we deserve because of it. It dictates what we see when we look in the mirror. It is the discontent that holds and guides us towards our perceived destinations. That is; perceived by Cornelius and not by ourselves. It tells us who we are, who we should love and who we must hate. It will dictate whether we are the class clown, the bookworm or the bully. Whether we like football or prefer dancing. It will even dictate whether we are fat, thin, muscular or athletic. If you try to dictate to it and choose your own path it will recognise your mutiny and put you right back to where you "belong". If you are large and wish to lose some weight you can make a good start, you may even gain *some* success, however, at some point Cornelius *will* correct this deviation from the set goal and your old largeness will return in full force. It will also provide you with new "reasons" as to why what you tried was futile and why you should be happy just the way you are, thus stifling any further insurrections. Or you may continually try – over and over again – for the rest of your life, always going so far but, ultimately, no further in this dream which always remained as such. Spurts of success that dissolves and becomes a pointless monotony over time. A character trait. Tales of constantly "giving-up" cigarettes for instance may give a person means to celebrate that, once upon a time, they "gave-up" for *three whole months!* Once they realise that action alone is clearly not working they give-up giving up and convince themselves that they actually like smoking. If you can't beat your addiction you may as well act like you gave yourself permission to enjoy your addiction.

Folly lays squarely with the fact that it is from the same old Cornelius that the conscious-mind draws its choices and therefore does nothing new to achieve a brand new possibility. Cornelius creates a world around the addiction that has beaten the decision making system, that supports the belief that the goal cannot be achieved, that supports the reasoning factor that makes up excuses as to why it actually doesn't want to be done, that weakens the resolve in the goal, disintegrates the importance of the goal and the status-quo has been re-established. Just another day at the office for Cornelius who must, at all costs, protect every prejudice and belief within the self-image.

These prejudices, beliefs and the self-image are all inadvertent and we may not even realise that they are there and that they are the reason, regardless of your many efforts, that you always seem to get the same or similar results. Within this fortitude lies a protective impulse that will become riled and may even lash out at anyone who contradicts what is believed within the stronghold as truth, even though we were not the ones to put that belief there ourselves and are unaware of why we are protecting such a belief - we protect it still. Like a flavourless crouton we were planted square into a soup of undisclosed flavour and soaked up what it was that surrounded us. Whether we preferred to be flavoured by another soup is not up to us. The flavour became you for you were in *it* and surrounded by it.

Cornelius may be our all-powerful hardwiring but he is not the intelligence behind the choices we make. That responsibility lies squarely with the conscious mind as this is the *thinking* mind. It thinks and has ideas and goals (all of which are under the intense scrutiny of Cornelius). It is the mind that *chooses* and can choose to do, say and act however it likes - as long as it is in accordance with what Cornelius deems correct. The Conscious mind has the unlimited power of imagination and can conjure brand new things previously unseen nor existed- all of which are drawn from memory and experience which is within the power of the intellect which, in turn, is within the power of Cornelius. Above all, the conscious mind holds the power of perception; to see things the way we see them- as so dictated by the experience of the great Cornelius. The conscious mind has the power to reason, to argue a point and to add new information to support that point - a point that Cornelius has deemed to the consciousness as an absolute fact regardless of proof. The fact is that we can always find the "proof" and "reasons" necessary to support whatever we are doing even if that reason is "because I said so" or "because I want to".

So Cornelius is ultimately responsible for the thoughts we think which finds expression in the things that we do which, in turn manifests as the things we have happening to us in our lives through our actions and our reactions.

The following illustration is based on the battle that takes place within us, as Cornelius utilises two vital sections of our brain that helps to re-engage us to the track of a goal set in place when deviation from the course occurs. These sections are responsible for the decision making and the fear that compels us to abandon our dreams and goals for the safety of comfort and contentment. The amygdala protects us by drawing us away from dangers and the ventromedial pre-frontal cortex is our decision making bureaucrat who sorts our priorities from all the information that pours in through our funnels and tells us which to do and which to not. The fears the amygdala protects us from are only perceived fears and may not actually harm us at all, a fear of buttons perhaps. It is not concerned with what is real or what is not, if the danger data has been set, then the amygdala will strive to protect us from this. Both sit at the front of the brain watching everything that passes through with a work-ethic that never rests. Their occupation is not to ask questions but to do what they do best without rest.

In our earliest habitat, from our first teachers, Cornelius became imbued with an X type programming. The X type programming was the culture of the habitat in which we grew. In the story of Tarzan, Viscount Greystoke was raised by apes thus his X type programming was that of wild apes. Our programming let us know when we were comfortable and content and when things were amiss. Our early environment, abundant with influence and examples of the X type, built a pattern of thinking, a set of beliefs and actions that enabled us to co-exist and survive within this X type environment with our other X-typers of whom we called our family. Here we learned who we were, who we should continue to be and what, under no circumstances, were we to ever accept. What we thought became what we did and what we did attracted to us the things that happened to us in our life.

If we were to one day be influenced by an outside force, and were to become infatuated with an idea, (let's call this other idea a Y type) we may intend on obtaining the things that we've noticed that come along with having a Y type idea. Yet, as it is something different to what we have always known and does not fit in with our current pattern of X thought process, what might happen to our state of comfort and what does Cornelius have to say about this new idea with regards to our, already established paradigm?

Cornelius' duty is always to protect us using any means necessary. Zero-tolerance. It is not our enemy yet it has no ability to make the distinction between good and bad, right or wrong. Cornelius knows only what it has been programmed to know and to do only what it has been programmed to do. Cornelius is our cybernetic system that attempts to keep us on destinies track. As far as it is concerned, this Y type idea is unknown and dangerous and can affect the status quo. In order to protect us, Cornelius ensures the senses become flooded with doubt. Doubt that a Y can ever exist in an X world. The Y idea is convincingly discarded as a ridiculous concept meant only for Y types and never for X types.

However the world is inundated with new ideas that are not of the nature we are familiar with and sometimes these can appear quite attractive. The grass is always greener, so to speak. So the Y idea once again returns and stays for a while longer within the X consciousness. An idea against the norm, attempting to infiltrate. This is where things can get aggressive... Cornelius, aware of the breach and dedicated to serving the set programming within the consciousness unleashes doubt, however this time the Y idea has returned stronger and more aware than before. Alas for Y, Cornelius is always prepared and releases a crippling swathe of fear into the consciousness. The pressure culminating between X and Y becomes too much to bear and the Y idea is rejected. Chased back from whence it came, Y disappears from the system thus restoring the X type life back to its former with no real harm incurred to the status quo.

When we have a new idea that goes against our usual pattern of behaviour, it is normal to become flooded with doubt and if the doubt is strong enough it will cause you to quit. If the doubt is questioned and we decided to continue on into this new and untrodden territory eventually it is normal to experience strong fear. The fear takes form as visions, scenarios play out in our mind's eye scarcely to any benefit thus the fear seems justified and reason is formed. Reasons to abandon the Y... Yet if you were to fight through the fear...

... Within time and now fully introduced to the conscious mind Y returns and is determined, this time, to succeed! It marches into the X conditioning and suggests a co-existence. Cornelius wants none of it and once again fires doubt with intent to force the Y idea out for good. Y, however, strafes; side-stepping the onslaught of the doubt-projectiles and juggernauts headfirst into Cornelius' counter-measure; *the wall of fear*. This wall of fear is the barrier that stops most of us dead in our tracks when we have the idea to attempt something brand new. If we can see past our doubts and move forward towards the new idea, be it a parachute jump, therapy or pursuing a new partner or job, it is the fear of what may happen next that is most commonly the thing that halts our forward motion. Fear of doing something we don't know how to. Fear of how we'll be perceived if we fail and fear of appearing ignorant may take hold and we can be stopped dead in our tracks. We may feel the need for familiarity and this can lead us straight back to where we started. We may not like it there but at least we know this place. At least here we can feel comfortable. Fear tells us that we can always turn back. Better the devil you know. Or...

... The Y idea; injured, bloody and brutalised stands yet tenacious. Cornelius, realising that the Y is becoming more powerful and is at risk of breaking through the wall of fear, feels that no other option stands available other than to activate the **red button** of tremulous *anxiety*.

Y, having defeated doubt yet still injured by fear walks gallantly into the subconscious space and stops, face-to-face with the great Cornelius, whose finger poised threateningly, hovering desperately yet purposefully over the red button of anxiety. "Don't do it Cornelius!" pleads Y, "Silence! I protect the X conditioning and I'll allow no intrusion from another possibility within this mind!" With his exclamation Cornelius displayed his determination with the descent of one bony finger, pressing on the red button of *anxiety* and opening the flood gates, inundating the mind itself with enough anxious energy to cause the body to shake and convulse and wash away the threat of Y occurring this time around. Cornelius has yet again won the day. The X type programming has taken some damage and is in shock yet is happy to be restored back to comfort.

Within the consciousness, hidden from detection and left behind from the battle, a small piece of Y remains... will it grow independently to fight one day for a place within the mental mainframe or shall it wither and fade with time to be seen or heard of nevermore?

Had Y succeeded in infiltrating the mind and moving through in spite of the anxiety that attacked with such ferocity, it would have temporarily controlled the functions of the conscious mind and may have allowed Y to dominate momentarily, causing the body to move in Y type motions and may have even achieved a Y type result! Think of it as a grain of sand infiltrating the shell of an oyster. The oyster fights to nullify the intruder. Consider the nacre of the oyster the fears, doubts and anxieties of the current programming swathing layer after layer over the intrusive grain of sand. And now consider this; that if the grain of sand remains within it will eventually and absolutely become a pearl. Iridescent with enriched newness. Pain would give way, once the agony subsides, to the beauty of a new existence.

The understanding of strife

WHEN A NEW IDEA IS introduced to us it is as natural as the truth that we were born and we will die that we will suffer through the intense states of doubt, fear and anxiety, however, if we can begin to condition ourselves to understand that these states are natural and that the body and mind must go through them in order to experience *any* innovative change, than we can be prepared for the occurrences as and when they appear instead of becoming surprised and traumatised by their visits. These states do not feel good, can make us believe we are journeying into dangerous situations and force us to abandon what it is we really want. If we're not aware of the nature of change, when these feelings arise it is natural that we will try to end them fast by the swiftest means necessary. The danger is very real of course but only to the old programming, which will do whatever it needs in order to survive. It is only logical when faced with strife and stress in any endeavour that the human response will naturally be to recede from the perceived cause. It is natural and logical yet it will prove counter-productive in the ascertainment of your goals as these may lay beyond your current programming.

The painful feelings are purposeful to the processes of tempering and resilience. It is the nature of growth through change that causes the pain and it is in the emergence through the other side that brings with it an insurmountable euphoria. When a sword is being strengthened it is placed into the fires and heated to an unbearable level. This creates instability within the blade. The instability makes it malleable and it is beaten continuously. When it is plunged into cold liquid it screams yet it emerges stronger than before. This is the process of all strengthening. But a strong blade without flexibility can be broken. The most effective swords are those of strength *and* flexibility. Able to withstand punishment of a high degree and flex back to standard – ready to go again. Strong yet flexible. Wise yet compassionate. This is the balance necessary to stand victorious in the great battles of life.

When the muscles grow in strength and size the fibres tear and the pain can be unbearable the first time it is experienced, yet it is necessary in the growth of strength. Those unaware of the value of the delayed onset of muscle soreness may think that they have caused themselves serious damage. They may think that they have done themselves wrong and they may quit. But knowing that the burn is natural to the strengthening of the muscle may even cause some to begin to enjoy the process.

You *will* feel doubt, you *will* feel fear and you *will* feel anxiety like you never have before; yet, should you persevere through these trappings and the guardians of the old, you will rise anew and you will experience a life that is beyond previous expectations. There are risks of course as there are risks in every course of life. How many times did you fall whilst learning to walk as a child? How many conversations did you have where you garbled through imperfect words? However, because you had not yet formed an ability to reason yourself away from the danger of failure you persevered in spite of continuous and dangerous tumblings and mumblings. If we were who we are now, learning to walk or talk with the conditioned reasoning we now hold, we may all be bound to laying dumb and immobile forever.

I once had an epiphany whilst looking at a tree stump that deserves recollection for the moment. The tree had obviously become unwanted by someone and they thought to cut it down yet, as I looked closer I noticed a tiny new life springing forth from the centre of the stump. The tree was displaying its determination to survive regardless of attempts from outside influences to stall or kill its progress.

As I sat looking at the springing of new life I realised that, although someone had tried to stop the trees growth, they had only succeeded in postponing its goal. The tree had its own mission and as long as its roots were alive beneath the surface it would live to strive skyward, its mission had been interrupted yet not foiled completely.

For those who had tried and failed, they would have had better luck had they had uprooted the entire stump thus ending the old goal entirely.

I realised that, in our own lives, if we had a programming within us that was uncongenial to our desired goals, that we may have been reaping results that we were not best pleased with, all was not lost! We were simply in motion along tracks that were of a predefined trajectory, set for us by others and if we wished for our destination to be changed to one of our own desire then we would have to do far more than to cut down our leaves and branches, the small changes in our lives, even cutting down the tree itself was not enough to stop the destinations ascent. We had to cut out our old programming from the root and plant in its stead a new seed, one of our own choosing. In his poem: " *The Coming of Wisdom with Time*", William Butler Yeats noted that "*Though the leaves are many, the root is one*", standing as a perfect illustration as to how we may have many trials and tribulations along our way yet they all stem from one root and the power to cultivate new roots by planting a new seed is only ever, through blameless discovery, within our own power. This will serve, depending on how you nurture the new seed, to eliminate your problems forever and offer instead opportunities for solutions. In other words, this will alter your perspective from one that looks for reasons as to *why we may not* to one that looks for possibilities as to *how we may!*

Building a house on a damaged and unsound foundation will eventually cause concern within the safety and stability of the construct. If a house is to be built anew, nothing will suffice other than a brand new, stronger and appropriate foundation to build upon.

This seems quite obvious and it is, however when I re-discovered this it was one of the most euphoric moments of my entire life and I set out to flood my mind with a new kind of thinking. One that *I* had decided to install and one that I had to upkeep in order for it to maintain its flourish as "knowing it" didn't mean that it was my natural programming. It didn't mean that I would now act and speak the way I wanted to be just because I watched a couple of seminars and read a few books. The limiting beliefs that were lain during my early years were still dominant regardless of what occurred on the outside. I sought to uproot the old limiting beliefs I held of myself and the world and campaigned to proliferate a brand new garden where my old weeds were once abundant. This, as aforementioned, was no easy feat and it is far from over for me. It can be painful and doubt regularly infiltrates. I have many dreams and nightmares of my time and life being wasted upon this mission to create and write my own story as it happened but for me this is an attack that I have become mostly aware will occur. This does nothing to numb the pain nor to pacify my nightmares and my fears sometimes threaten to reap away my precious and hard earned cultivation. I fear sometimes what friends will think of the drastic change that I am trying to develop in my life. I fear my family and I even fear people I don't know and what they would think of me. However, due to my many great teachers from the past and present, I am prepared and know the nature and the why of the struggles I face. I knew that the fear was coming and had my own counter measures with regards to dealing with them when they reared their heads.

Success is always right in front of you. Gaining it simply means clearing away the debris that is in your way. Sometimes the debris is too heavy to lift alone and you may need help to remove it but the success is always there, waiting for you to clear the path.

Upon beginning my endeavour I had no money and a low income that was barely enough to pay my outgoings. I felt trapped and as though I needed more money now. I needed change now. I struggled whilst writing this book to keep financial ends together, stress threatened to beat within my chest at every hour of the day. But something was different within me. I knew that I was harvesting the good crops that I had sown long ago so I persevered in sowing for the new seasons of the future *right now* in spite of the demands for money and time. In spite of the seemingly impossible situation and the machinations that society had supposedly planned for me, I remembered the words of one of my great teachers; Booker T. Washington, when he had just returned from a long journey on foot and was told immediately that he had to set off again as there was the possibility of a businessman who may be interested in investing in his school:

"He listened with some degree of interest to what I had to say, but did not give me anything. I could not help having the feeling that, in a measure, the three hours that I had spent in seeing him had been thrown away. Still, I had followed my usual rule of doing my duty. If I had not seen him, I should have felt unhappy over neglect of duty."

Booker T Washington had a work ethic to behold and had imbued within himself the nature to do his duty regardless of the outcome. In this particular case Mr. Washington's hard work and diligence paid off as the businessman decided to pay him a substantial sum quite some time after his visit. In actual fact his ethic to "do the work" *always* paid off. By planting the seed on that day in spite of his doubts and feelings, in spite of what seemed obvious, he later reaped the harvest, as his legacy continues to do so to this very day, of what he had sown.

For one such as myself, creating a life of my own design was the greatest thing I could have ever imagined to achieve due to the fact that I had been fully hypnotised to the belief that we can only move forward based on the achievements and actions of the past and of our present circumstance. I once wrote in an old diary: *"What is my incentive, if failure is the only outcome?"* This new revelation meant that my past was now history and that my future would only be determined by my present, of which I was now fully in control of and therefore would only be determined by my present actions and reactions to present occurrences. That didn't mean that everything that happened was my choice. I didn't want to have debts up to my ears and little earnings to pay it back or to fund my projects, but my reactions were my choices. I was in control. I was winning.

"I was tired, I was hungry, I was everything but discouraged"
Booker T. Washington

I was one of the many who became so obsessed and upset with the past that I forgot completely how I was creating my problems with my present actions which were influenced by my past which in turn created my future. Now my present actions were created by, not my regrets of the past but my wishes and goals of the future.

A freeing moment indeed and a power that can be utilised by any.

When planting a seed, remember that for a long season all you will see is nothing but so much dirt. The toil will be hard but the knowledge of what you have planted and what you continue to nurture will, in its time and if nurtured correctly, produce the harvest of your choosing.

Therefore we must be aware of the seeds we are planting every day. It is far easier to plant a seed of destruction and negativity as these things need no conscious nurturing. As the weeds grow so will your hate and discontent, burrowing deep and reaching high, engulfing all that you see. Planting a seed of love requires care and attention in every moment awake and in slumber.

Be very aware of who you are and what you intend - for what you sow you will most surely, either sooner or later, be sure to reap.

Although the elements had welded the frozen, heavy lashes of his eyelids closed, he slowly rubbed them open with the back of an ice-cold, gloved hand. Opening his eyes felt as though he were tearing brand-new slits with which to see and through fazed vision he realised that the sun was setting. Laboriously, desperately heaving and rolling himself to a crawling position, Kaden searched in a frenzy for his prize, every muscle burned with each movement until finally his vision met with what had hitherto been but a reverie to him. Something that was spoken of by many yet eyes lain by none. The rose stood strong moving to and fro with the wind, inviting, gesticulating. It seemed to call to Kaden and readily he answered.

Crawling with haste, breath heaving loudly and grunting petulantly, he dragged himself up to the rose. As though through hypnosis, Kaden about reached out his hand to touch it. Snapping back to reality he quickly pulled his hand back, stopping for a moment in wonder to what he had almost done. Fumbling behind him for his satchel, he pulled forth the severed, greyed hand of Titus! Placing his palm on its back he closed his fist, and in turn, clenched the cleaved, dead fist of Titus around the rose. No blood let from the appendage as Kaden slowly lifted and plucked the rose from its root, thus, in that moment, its gift had been relinquished. Kaden had achieved his purpose with careful and dutiful precision.

Creating Our Environment

Sensory Perfection

AS THE PIERCING SCREAM INSTIGATES thoughts of terror and the engulfing sound of an explosion deviates hope, does the sound of a child's laughter and the tiny bird's spring song bring thoughts of peace and future promise. As the touch of our beloved's warmth through soft skin and our fingers through their silken hair bring feelings of bliss, does the feeling of cold steel across the throat and the tight grip across the wrist translate to a tight constricting grip within the heart. As the taste of something sweet upon our lips is pleasing, as is the dripping of blood down the throat frightening and worrying. As does the sight of a green expanse in the bright sun-kissed sky bring feelings of calm and the sight of beauty bring thoughts of excitement does the site of a baron and burned out wasteland bring unease and that of a powerful stranger in our way bring thoughts of dismay. The sensory functions are the partners to our two minds; the conscious, thinking mind and the unconscious, unthinking mind: Cornelius.

The sensory functions, the five funnels as we spoke of, are vital to the state of vibration we find ourselves in at any time. When our state of vibration is harmonious and we *feel* good, this simply means that all of the stimulants that Cornelius has deemed pleasing and calming to us are being satisfied. Yet this is purely subjective as satisfaction is a psychological quality. There are those who live for the macabre and depravity. To these, the aforementioned are adverse in their stimulations and would leave the host in a state of disharmony until the senses could be satisfied by dark and depraved stimulants, thus returning the state of vibration back to one that is accepted as normal and comfortable.

This is the nature of the sub-conscious mind we have named Cornelius. To seek to maintain the state of harmony through external stimuli for whatever has been set as normal within the first six to eight years of life, regardless of what "normal" may have been. Deviation from this state creates disharmonious vibrations within the body. Dis-comfort and disarray ensues until the flailing armed robot is returned to a seated, calm and happy Buddha, by Cornelius, who sought the corrective stimuli necessary to reinstate internal order. When in a state of intense disharmony the body will shake and tremor, displaying the vibrations for all to see.

If Cornelius holds the status, the programming, the blueprint, the ideal – whatever it may be called – for the norm that must be met throughout our lives then why does such chaos and doubt ensue so often? Thus is the quiet battle of the two-minds.

In the days of us living as purely sub-conscious beings, Cornelius had the duty of formatting all of the stimuli that entered through the funnels into ideals for us. Tirelessly he listened and gathered. Sorting all of the information that entered, Cornelius cultivated a plan of progression for life and the stuff-external, the stimuli, which would most effectively appropriate this plan of progression. With not a pause nor distraction, Cornelius created the cybernetics and continued to do so as the conscious mind began to form. This became the blueprint, the MAP to the journey (Motivation-Attitude/Association-Purpose/Perception) as such, that Cornelius would strive to maintain course for, for the entirety of the lifespan. Eventually the conscious mind, now fully formed and much like the curious wolf cub of Jack London's classic novel "White Fang", set out into this world, to discover the joys and trials. Discovering and growing. The conscious mind would see and hear, taste, smell and touch all manner of things. It would decide what was right and what was wrong based on the former data input installed by Cornelius and anything that did not suit the programming caused disharmony and thus discomfort and the consciousness veered away, back to harmony. Back to comfort. Back to the way things were planned from the beginning.

At some point the consciousness, naturally of a more curious nature than Cornelius (who is the master of reflex and automation), garners ideas, dreams and hopes that do not fall pari passu with the plans set by Cornelius. Yet, at this stage, Cornelius has no need to show any concern as this is a natural trait of the curious mind. Soon, as the curiosity of this new idea attracts closer, new stimuli will be encountered and will set the body into discord. Eventually the conscious mind will seek harmonious stimuli to return the feeling of safety and comfort and draw away from the dream. Cornelius understands that, if this idea persists in the consciousness things *can* become quite difficult.

Back in the conscious mind, and away from the prying eyes of Cornelius in the sub-conscious, another, brand new blueprint is being formulated. A plan for the future that is different than the one deep in the vaults of the sub-conscious. The consciousness seeks stimuli for this new goal, this new plan for life, but the new stimulus hurts. It causes doubt and pain which is not pleasing. It is of a different vibration that the old is not accustomed to.

Now housed internally are two agendas. Two separate blueprints of purpose for the way that life *should* be. One created for you arduously by Cornelius and one by the consciousness of the thinking mind. One is called a dream and the other a reality. One is cybernetic (automatically set in motion) and the other is cultivated (worked on) and only one will ever make it to the end.

Thus moves the cycle: our experience creates our expectations and our expectations create our experiences. We become caught in this cycle of experience and expectancy like the climbing of a perpetual ladder in a nightmare that we cannot wake from.

Purpose, nurture and stimuli

I HAVE SAID THAT SATISFACTION is a psychological quality, thus what satisfies us is based on what we have been internally programmed to accept. Anything else is unacceptable and deemed as negative stimuli to the cause. From birth all stimuli was set for us; this was termed as *culture* to which we innately veer towards. We need never search for this as, if we stand unmoving, it will surely come to us, or we unconsciously scan all environmental areas continually to provide sustenance to our comfort. Our cultural stimuli. Yet if we were to dare to dream, to veer from the program, this new alien stimuli would not just naturally be there, it will *not* come to us and we would not naturally scan for its presence. We would need to cultivate knowledge of it and begin to seek it out *actively* and we would have to retrain ourselves to stand up to the task. For as this is sought, and we travel beyond the realms of our innate frequency, our state of vibration will naturally alter, becoming something that we don't recognise nor do we feel equipped to handle. Fear and doubt then draws us back to a frequency that does not bring fear and doubt and we are thus set back on the track set by Cornelius.

So is it just then a process of push on or give up? The means adopted by Cornelius, adopted by the trees and adopted by every living thing on this planet are these weapons: "purpose", "nurture" and "stimuli".

Nurture is simply covert teaching.

Everything that lives on our beautiful and mysterious planet has a purpose and consistently seeks adequate stimulus to meet this purpose. The acorn has its purpose in becoming an oak tree but it is not one. It is an acorn.

It must seek the things needed to stimulate its journey. If it is starved of its stimuli it is starved of its ability to succeed in its purpose. The nurture in this case would be the effects the world imposes upon the seeds journey to fulfil its course. We too had a seed and the stimuli to stay this course. Where we differ from the acorn lays in our *consciousness*. The acorn is *set* to become a tree and to seek stimuli as to such ends, unless interfered with. The acorn has no interest in becoming anything else but an oak tree. We too have the seed, the purpose and the stimuli yet, the consciousness, unique in its design, has the ability to become inspired. To feel and to dream. Above all else, the consciousness has the ability to *plant brand new seeds*. In spite of the purpose posed and slaved over by Cornelius, we have the unique ability to plant a new idea of new purposes. Ideas to fly or to travel through space and time or to change who we once were. We have the ability, within the conscious mind, to create and to design a new plan. A new purpose.

Yet this does nothing to do away with the old purpose set by Cornelius. It does nothing to stifle the stimulants placed in your environment to consistently correct your deviation. Cornelius is far from worried as it understands fully the nature of the consciousness. It understands that the consciousness is excited and will become overwhelmed with possibilities. Possibility after possibility inundates the consciousness and eventually confusion sets in as, although all possibility is abundant, purpose has been left by the wayside. The purpose is the reason and if the "why" is weak than so shall be the resolve to attain that "why".

> *"He who has a why to live for can bear almost any how"*
> Friedrich Nietzsche

The purpose serves to *drive* you to your *chosen* possibility, without which there can be no movement. A car with no drive serves not its own purpose but the chosen purpose of others. Perhaps as scrap. To dream for the human is completely natural however, those who fulfilled their dreams were those who found a strong purpose for doing so. Not once! But consistently. If we fail to establish a solid purpose that is clear and specific to us, more than anything else, we have no hope in overcoming the obstacles that we *will* encounter along the way. These will be obstacles that we *ourselves* have stepped up to in order to pass through on to a higher level, and will cause much disruption to the vibratory frequency that we have become used to. We will find moving toward these new vibrations so very uncomfortable yet, because we ourselves have stepped to them and there is no one who holds us to the heat, *we* can choose to step away, right back to a harmonious frequency, which is exactly what we do if we do not have a purpose that we are emotionally connected to. A purpose that means everything to us.

To become the one who we *need* to be in order to face the heat, we must constantly stimulate ourselves to this end. If we are to build our physicality to super muscularity we would create playlists to work out to, buy appropriate gear for the home, read books on the subject, consume what is necessary to feed our bodies to this end and possibly subscribe to a gym and hire a personal trainer. We would watch videos and movies and listen to appropriate advice. If someone tells us that big muscles are stupid we don't listen. We would look into the mirror to reflect upon our progress and the changes we've made. We *surround* ourselves with the stimulants that will move us forward, constant bombardments of who and what it is that we are trying to achieve and we work tirelessly for hours and days and months on end. When the muscle burns we learn that it is *supposed* to burn. We learn that this is natural to the struggle and we come to love the burn. When we can barely move we learn about the Delayed Onset of Muscle Soreness (D.O.M.S) in which the fibres of the muscles break apart only to be fused together again stronger and thicker, we accept that it is a part of the journey and fear it no more. We create slogans as such: "Go Hard or Go Home!", "No

Pain No Gain!", "Two More!" in order to egg us on continuously. We do this and we know this very well.

I have used this example to demonstrate the point as it comes from a perspective of the physical which is a viewpoint more easily understood by us all. Yet the principle for attaining a life of our design, be it whatever we may, is the exact same one. Create a vision for your dream, give it a purpose that you will fight for and set the stimulants everywhere that will pressure you to its manifestation. Before we have muscles we have none yet in time the old body is a memory and a new muscular one stands - poised majestically in its stead.

Depression; the deep feeling of a lack of purpose and control in one's own life. A terrible feeling of hopelessness for another way of living purposefully. This can be due to the two agendas within us that we never took ownership of. The lack of purpose and control can stem from following one agenda over the other. One that we did not consciously choose. Many very wealthy people still suffer from depression as they found themselves pursuing a life that didn't fit their *ideal* of how life *should* be. "Should" being an implication that things are not the way they are *meant* to be causes us to believe that something then *must* be wrong. Perhaps they felt they *should* be a lawyer or a teacher because that's what their parent wanted them to be. Maybe being a parent was the dream of the parents to be Grandparents someday and letting them down was impermissible. Perhaps, unknowingly, their purpose was always to fulfil someone else's purpose and to satisfy and please another to the neglect of their own dreams, wishes and goals.

When creating an ideal for our life's journey we must be clear. We will muster many ideals. We will want to be an actor and a fireman and an astronaut also, yet we must choose and be clear and then create a strong vision and purpose to see it to its fulfilment.

As you derive a strong purpose to your cultivated thought, set up all around you, designed to engage each sensory function, stimuli to achieve your means. Remove distractions that threaten to pull you off course and prepare for the oncoming burn with glee.

Benjamin Fairbairn

The Spectrums of Experience

WHEN WE WERE BABIES WE were vulnerable and needed taking care of. When we become old the same becomes true. When we are suffering intensely there is a pain in our chest and bellies and we cannot stop the tears flowing. When we experience intense euphoria the same becomes true. Both ends of the spectrum are paradoxical points along the same line of experience and the point of balance exists in the fulcrum. Spectrums are energy and energy is and always is absolutely everything. All we experience is energy vibrating at different frequencies along the line of a spectrum.

A spectrum is the vibrating energy of a particular experience where all possibilities lay. It is a line on which absolutely everything falls and by understanding the nature of the spectrums we can *begin* to understand how things like failure, pain, suffering, success, joy and misery are all many levels of the same spectrum. This is useful to understand because, as we do, we can realise that we are never distanced from the ability to change our state but are only ever at different frequencies of the very same. Once we can establish where the fulcrum of action lays then we can begin to see just how we can veer from a choice with not very beneficial consequences to choices that bring us what we wish. Theology teaches us that everything comes from something and goes to something else and was brought into manifestation by a greater being who has always been. Therefore everything that has always been and ever will be has always been around in one form or another. Science teaches us that the law of the conservation of energy means that nothing ever disappears, it only ever changes form and becomes the use of something else. Therefore nothing is ever actually created or destroyed and everything simply changes its course of energy to a different function. It seems to my understanding that science and theology are in complete and unanimous agreement and the only difference is the name that things are given. What is also stated is that everything that is energy is constantly in a *consistent* state of vibration. If the spectrum of everything is energy then where we are placed on that spectrum at any given time *must* be our level of vibration. The frequency that we are in.

$\mathcal{B}$alance

FOR INSTANCE, WE COULD PLACE a balance beam on a pivot and when the beam is straight the pivot can be called "the zero point", anything to the right can be positive with perfect bliss at its tip. Anything to the left can be considered negative with absolute suffering at its tip. If we are on the zero point all is well. There is no imbalance and there is no danger. The safest thing to do would seem to be to stay unmoving, yet by not moving, naturally you will not go anywhere nor experience anything. You may look over at the other sides but moving will cause an imbalance so you stay put. The other option is to sit on one tip but this is impossible as to sit on the right tip would be absolute euphoria and the left tip would mean absolute suffering. Absolutes in either end is imbalance. Alternatively if we understand that action is the key to experience and that means that sometimes, by moving along the line, we'll experience suffering and sometimes we'll experience bliss we will attain a good understanding as to what the balance of life is like. However, when we feel that we are moving too close to the edge we know that, in order to regain balance, we will need to begin moving back to balance. This is a crude demonstration yet it serves to say that the spectrum of life is left to us to control and experience its balance. No one ever tips our scales to the point where we cannot regain our balance by recognising our own position and re-adjusting accordingly.

We may at different times fall into different spaces and places on the spectrum yet we are always a part of it, moving ceaselessly like a bubble in a spirit level telling exactly (if we are to be aware of it) where we are at any given time. Suffering can slide off into fear and a perpetual grief or can slide the other way to learning and a forward movement into freedom and attainment. If we find ourselves in poverty and lack we know that there are certain actions that we can take to move into the side of wealth and prosperity. But this never "just happens". We have to move.

How we arm ourselves to deal with the spectrums of life is completely up to us. We all are born of this earth and the earth's natural laws are the same and as accessible to one as is to the other. True that some of this worlds inhabitants are born into situations and states that do not offer much chance for survival or for improvement of any kind. Hope is at an all-time minimal for some, this is not however the case for us. We have suffered and we have ourselves *caused* much suffering, we have hurt and been hurt, yet we now find ourselves at a place where we can find strength on the spectrum of our own lives. We can also understand that if we are not moving toward one direction we can be sure that we can only be moving in the other. Now we are able to realise that each move we make is a move on the spectrum of *choice* toward or away from our intentions at any given time and this is of vital importance.

Our speech can be a movement towards usefulness, to inform and inspire or a descent into uselessness through the spreading of rumours, lies and propaganda.

Our actions can be used to aid and to build and caress or it can be used idly or to demolish and cause harm.

Our thoughts can bring hope and newness or it can perpetuate fear, hatred and suffering.

A choice in one direction imbibes in euphoric success and magical attainment and a choice in the other can bring blame, suffering and ultimately, an absolute waste of all human potential. The choice is always ours. The responsibility is never out of our hands no matter how difficult things may seem. Every step of the way, regardless of the illusions of hopelessness that may be heavy and penetrating, we are the only power in our lives with the immeasurable opportunity to afflict our own unique impact upon this magical planet. Thus; life and our future becomes fertile instead of futile - potent instead of putrid. Whether we are aware of it or not, everything we do is a seed and the seed will flourish.

Kaden had a dream and a vision. He also devised a plan of acquisition. Unfortunately, he chose to inflict pain and sacrifice life in order to gain his goals. Everything we do, always comes back to us in one way or another.

Not yet a week had passed by since his weary feet had touched upon the ground and the pain reverberated through his bones and joints still, like millions of tiny hammers, banging away within his marrow. His descent was a lengthy, soul blistering venture that had almost taken everything from him and yet, it was done... At an un-mentionable cost, yet still it was done. If there was nothing else to be claimed of Kaden you could most assuredly claim him tenacious and if he was hard to kill before he had now crowned himself: *immortal*.

The rose sat lone on a mantle of old, dark oak in a thick glass jar which reflected the flames that burned within the fire-place. The warmth of the room had to contend with the coldness that sat in his heart. A method he had devised in order to be able to live with the heinous act that crawled under his skin. During his descent he had become desperate and thoughts had crept to mind to leap from where he was, after all, with immortality flowing though him, he would yet survive would he not? He chose against discovery as he did not know exactly when the rose would bequeath its magic. Was it gradual or immediate? Once hitting the ground would his bone and sinew snap and form back into previous shape or would he be cursed to live within a mangled and broken frame until the end of time? It was better that he use his new prize wisely and uncover its uses slowly over time as he now had decidedly enough time to learn. The fire-place grumbled and spat with a flame which emitted a welcoming blanket of heat throughout the cottage, like a servant warrior fighting back the cold which tried to force its way in from outside. Kaden slouched alone, feet on stool, wine in hand, head hung forward, chin-to-chest, and eyes furrowed with faux focus in front of the fire and mused. Staring into the faces within his mind of the towns-folk from which he had expected reverence yet instead was reaping from them a vehemence of the utmost distaste. He had achieved that which none hitherto had dared dream, yet when he arrived back to the town he was vilified for returning minus Titus. "Titus, my good friend" he had thought "were it not for you I would not be here to enjoy eternity's secrets. I would be nothing more than *everyone else* here in this god-forsaken place. Destined to be forgotten with all who dwell here within. Nothing more than the dirt to which they must return. But not I", Kaden faux laughed, "Titus my friend, I owe it all to you. And to you I raise a toast... TO TITUS!" Once he finished the contents of the glass, Kaden, who was now quite high-spirited, began to pour and fill his glass once more with celebratory wine "... and to me!" as he had done every day since his descent. Not one wished to congratulate him for his miraculous return. Miraculous at the expense of the good Titus. "My friend Titus, with whom I jostled with as a child. With whom I shared those precious final moments, I know you would understand what I had to do, yet were I to tell you? How could I? No, this is our prize. The *both* of us! TO US!"

The wife and child of Titus had, days before, bore upon Kaden's door, to ask how he could live with himself knowing that he drew Titus away from his family to his final fate... If only they knew how true they were.

Kaden's zealous slurping from his cup was disturbed abruptly by the strange rubbing against the wood of his door from the outside. He paused and focused his ear to hear the rubbing and dragging of cloth and soft, wet, sodden leather against the door. "Oh? Have you not told me enough what is in your hearts of me? Go!" Yelled Kaden to the intruder unseen, "You have all expressed clearly enough! I care not... Leave me! Go." To which he commenced the emptying of his cup down his chin, chest and, to some degree, his throat... Yet the rubbing continued which infuriated Kaden to his feet; 'I say now go!' His cup, emptied of its content now flung through the air and became pieces against the door of which, on the other side and without pause the sound of leather rubbing and thudding upon the wood, steadily persisted.

Benjamin Fairbairn

The Problem with Problems

FOR SOME PEOPLE IN THIS world problems are the only thing that holds them together. If they didn't have the problems that they consider "theirs" it seems that they would fall to pieces. It is the only thing that falls from their lips when they speak and the only thing that seeps from their minds when they stop speaking. They appear to be there in front of our eyes but they never actually are. They are either in the past, grousing over happenings now gone or in the future, consternating in fear over happenings not yet occurred. Like the offal inside the stomach bag of haggis, they are of themselves and wrapped up inside themselves.

For those of us who train to cultivate the master-skill, problems become obscure but not because they disappear from life completely. They become obscure because the anatomy of the problem itself is perceived much differently. It is perceived in such a different light that it augments what is usually called "problem" into something completely different.

A problem can be seen as something unwelcome or harmful to us or they can be seen as an unexpected opportunity for something else to begin.

It would seem that the problem with problems is that we have been overly conditioned to expect our lives to be without them which causes us to feel *guilty* for having them. We feel distracted and poorly treated when presented with "problems" and we begin to think that something must be wrong if we experience them in our lives. We become envious over other people who don't seem to have the problems that we do and we begin to feel unable to deal with a life that has so many "problems". When this happens these "problems" just become bigger, badder and way more ferocious. How many problems do you have in your life at this moment? Do you think that your life would be better off without them? The circumstances we label as "problems" never go away and if we would wish to be free of their burdensome effect on our lives then we have to alter the way we are looking at them. We can never hope to alter the fact that challenge in life exists and will always exist, however we can always alter the way we perceive these challenges.

"I have learned that success is to be measured not so much by the position that one has reached in life as by the obstacles which he has overcome while trying to succeed."

Booker T. Washington

The Whisperings of Angels

The Quality of Resilience

IT WOULD SEEM THAT THE purpose of life's conditioning is in the augmentation of the perception we hold of the circumstances in our lives. Sometimes we believe that, if we are not agreeable to the circumstance that we have in life, we can go about complaining or trying to change the circumstance within the moment. What might be more useful to the situation would be to realise that our current circumstance is nothing more than our past's consequence occurring right now in the present moment. It is in the manner with which we choose to deal with this consequence that will subsequently create *tomorrow's* circumstance. It is vital to understand that we are only ever experiencing the now and that fretting about the past or worrying about the future causes us to miss the point completely. The point of which is this: in order to give promise to the present moment we must always be aware of being present in the moment. We can only experience the future as it becomes the present moment. Everything else is a fabrication created in our heads. It is what we choose to do right now that will determine where we stand in the future. Thus it makes sense to me that, if we are unhappy with an occurrence in the present moment that we will look deeply as to why we are seeing something that cannot be augmented to a beneficial state? This is the purpose of resilience. Resilience fuels our diligence and without either we will not veer from the negative frequency where we currently reside on the spectrum of experience.

Your life is as easy as you are consciously aware that all problems are *nothing* but possible solutions for another way and all it ever takes is a *shift* in the way we see things to truly get the best out of life. My life today is a vast divergence from the misery in which I used to dwell, not because life around me has changed particularly but because my conscious awareness of life has augmented and developed beyond what it was. Issues and occurrences appear and people may say "how will you deal with this Benjamin?" to which I am likely to reply "with gusto!" I came to realise at some crucial point that perception was subjective and that if I had the idea that life was terrible then I could do one of two things; I could either changes all of the terrible things that was happening around me, one by one, or I could change my perception of those things. Whilst doing so, I knew I would have to fortify a conditioning of resilience to be able to weather the storm that comes with change.

The Quality of Accountability

"PROBLEMS" OF ANY ILK HOLDS within it the possibility of imbuing those who recognise its nature with powers that lead to more powers and more success. In order to relinquish the great lessons our "problems" have to offer we must first embrace the quality of accountability for each circumstance of our lives, and this requires a maturity and wisdom that is not bound by age. Accountability is the knowledge that we alone are responsible for the effects that stem from the causes in our lives and is a quality that can be nurtured into our children which will promise to release their future from the bonds of suffering and instead, open to them to the limitless opportunities that comes with being consciously alive. They will not suffer their future as they will understand and embrace the fact that change is a natural occurrence in life. Change occurs whether we wish it to or not. Whether we are ready for it or not and this is not tantamount to life being "against" us. We suffer our own problems by attempting to stifle the change, to hold the clock back and to keep things just the way they are. We are always either moving forward in progression or backward in regression. This is a natural law that we would benefit from realising in order to halt us from suffering our problems any further. The real problems occur when we decide it is our mission to chase away the inertia. We chase and chase until we become tired and drained and finally realise that we have been chasing something that just doesn't exist in life. Before we know it, we see that we have, in the midst of our wild-goose chase, become older and slower and we embrace blame. But blame is not is not reserved for the children who don't know better and the aged who didn't do better; blame is plentiful and there will always be enough for everybody.

The Whisperings of Angels

The Inflammation of Blame in Life

WHEN WE SUDDENLY DISCOVER THAT our way of thinking is not quite producing the results that we thought they would, there can be little time spent upon finding someone to blame if we're intent on walking a greater path. We will always find people to point our cragged finger at and we'd probably be correct in our accusation of where our teachings came from, however that is not the point for those who are looking to cultivate the master-skill. To look to do something better for themselves. Blame is simply the word used to deter responsibility and deflect accountability. We may not be responsible for the programming we received as children, however, as soon as we became old enough to think for ourselves, we became the ones responsible as to whether or not we chose to move forward with our limiting beliefs. We are also the only ones who stands responsible for making the appropriate changes.

There has never been a wise man or woman throughout our history who has tried to work against the laws of nature. Innovation can be experienced and enjoyed when we work *together* with nature's laws instead of trying to work against them. There has never lived an inspirational figure who has been known to refract blame away from themselves. We have seen actions and accomplishments of the greatest examples of human-kind pass through century and decade and transcend death because they held their fates in their own hands and were prepared to fight for their right to affect their lives however they would choose to, even in the face of the most unspeakable odds.

Success is preparation for everything and nothing in particular whilst being open, aware and functioning with life's constant motion. It will always be up to the individual as to whether they use this one throw at life to be victim to the apparitions of strife that they feed and suffer, or whether they will embrace this unique opportunity that so many do not have.

Nothing is ours or here but everything is passing through. A great conveyer belt of experience that becomes something new within every moment. Problems are nothing but our altered *perceptions* of the passing through and our attachments to the passing through. We no more belong to the problems we consider "ours" than they belong to us.

The relationship and ownership we hold to these circumstances do not come from clear and happy minds. They stem from a chain of suffering that exists within the consciousness and is held as a belief to protect within the sub consciousness. Like an old basement full of horrors that we have locked tight with a key that only we hold. A basement that we cannot bear to go down and rifle through, not even for the sake of cleaning out. To venture into this basement of suffering would put our whole lives at risk... Or so we tell ourselves. The basement is just full of old nonsense and the moment we can clear it out the more space we will have for the light to shine through.

Kaden knew something was amiss as he stood now staring at the door of his abode... There was a plunge of pressure within his solar-plexus and his jugular veins filled with ache. As he stared at the door, which persisted its torment, a sharp mohawk of pain reverberated through his cranium and a slab of ice sat in his stomach.

Kaden was not an easy man to scare and yet, as he stood there staring at the door, for some reason, he was afraid. The rubbing of sodden leather against the wood of his door continued. "LEAVE ME ALONE!" This scream beat the air with multiple frequencies and hurt Kaden's throat and made his muscles tremble as he fell to his knees... but it seemed to work. The rubbing and thudding had finally, unbelievably ceased...

The Whisperings of Angels

The Capacity for Tolerance

THE CAPACITY FOR TOLERANCE IS not one that any would immediately associate with humanity due to the fact that it has made intolerance an ongoing staple characteristic throughout its history. Had John Harrison known, when he devised the first method of accurate navigation through the discovery of calculable longitude, that the power he aided to bestow on this world would have been used to spread intolerance, death and the gratuitous slaughter of millions, perhaps he would have thought twice. Or perhaps in his mind he was devising a tool to use for the mission of good throughout the world? A means to help and love and coadunate? Perhaps, although perhaps this would have been seen as a sign of weakness to other lands. Is intolerance then a form of protection? Does the phrase: "*only the strong survive*" really mean: only those survive who chooses to kills first? Could intolerance be a method then of paving the future with peace through the fear of war, death and destruction? As the jihadists claim to be fearless in their striving to rid the world of the infidel then they are either lying, unaware of their fear or there is another fuel for intolerance other than that of fear. There is the saying that: every villain is a hero through their own eyes and the eyes of their followers. Is righteousness then nothing more than the majority opinion? And does this mean that all those who remain fall into the bucket of wrong opinions? To answer the question of intolerance we would first have to answer the question: "is our belief the right one? If so, how do we defend it?" Every single person has a belief even if you choose to believe nothing. You also have the right to defend your belief, however, if your belief is not that of the majority, you had better get ready for a fight. Alternatively you could just tolerate your rights being overthrown.

It would seem that we have a set standard for our lives – as mentioned in previous chapters – whether we are aware of them or not and we tend to protect it to the greatest of our abilities. Our right to protect anyone from removing this standard is just. We can muster powers from unforeseen corners when our standards are threatened and we will not tolerate anything trying to control us other than that which we allow to, whether we are also aware of this or not. The standards of our lives are the things that creep in through an uninvited loophole of nature's law; the law that created our Cornelius which houses the image we hold of ourselves. This tells us what we are worth and what we cannot exist without. It creates our esteem and tells us that, without these certain things our lives will be intolerable and this gives us the power to tolerate. However, these "certain things" naturally change within different times of our lives and tolerance, as with everything, has its own spectrum. There is the spouse who tolerates abuse and violence towards themselves and allows abuse and violence to befall others. Tolerance in this case is useless and harmful and on the opposite end of this spectrum is the intolerance of any outside help; any possible solution away from the abuse. If you were to intervene a person beating their pet dog the dog would most surely attack you in defence of its owner, such is the tolerance of abuse and intolerance of outside intervention.

We choose what we tolerate by what we expect from the individual others. The standards we hold of them, of our perceptions to the outside and of ourselves. Tolerance and intolerance is never mastered as we are consistently changing throughout every moment of our lives, thus we can never "complete" the work on what is considered "us". What is necessary is to learn a method of consistent maintenance through the power of awareness which constantly adjusts our levels of tolerance to-and-fro based on what we are feeling within in each moment... Like a spirit level on a ship in a storm. How easy is it to keep that bubble level all the time? Well, who said anything about easy?

Tolerance and control

COULD IT BE POSSIBLE THAT our tendencies towards intolerance may be down to our own struggle for control? Within our lives we tend to syphon control from some places and completely forego it in others and those who are lacking intention with their goals take control wherever it is easiest, safest and given. This could mean that in the place of control over the things that can take a bit more time and discipline, we would instead find control in the things that are of no challenge and are easily taken like over the vulnerable, the weaker and those unable to respond. We may become aggressive to show that we are in control of our actions. We may become harsh and difficult to deal with and, as no one can deal with us, we would take some sort of pride in the knowledge that no one has the power to *control* us. We may also be a submissive character that is constantly dominated by others and our tolerance to this dominance could be our way of fooling ourselves that we are actually in control. That we're being dominated because we're *allowing* them to. That we are *choosing* to be peaceful by not being confrontational. The actuality would be that we are frightened by the lack of control we are missing over the things that really matter in our lives. We may have no idea how to handle real powers of society like our finances, the company we keep or our status both socially and domestically or the things that really matter in this world like being at one with our hearts and our minds, being vulnerable and loving towards others and being open and free. We may have no idea of what we want or who we are in the ocean of chaos. We may feel vulnerable, scared and powerless and therefore find power in *fabricating* power through making others feel helpless, making others cower and making a big noise that no one can quiet.

Real control comes from knowing ones intention, giving one's self a command and having the discipline to see it through to completion. It comes from recognising our ignorance and embracing it to be at one with the lessons that the world is continually providing. It means shutting our mouths and opening our hearts. It comes from realising our vulnerabilities and weaknesses and finding the strength within to face them every day and to seek new ways to empower one's self through embracing ones vulnerability. Real control is on a spectrum, just like everything and it will bring peace to know that sometimes we feel in control and sometimes we just don't and that's ok. It comes from realising that we can only control our own responses, thoughts and deeds and no one else's and that things are always going to happen in this world that will make us feel less than strong, less than happy and less than complete yet we do not have to struggle to change these things but to only respond with the greatest self that we can possibly muster in every given moment.

There is a saying that selfishness is not living your life the way you want to – selfishness is expecting others to live their lives the way you want them to. Selfishness is in the expectancy that everybody *must* tolerate you. Selfishness is expecting everybody to like you and love you and care for you. It's not that you don't deserve these things, I believe that we all do, however if you spend your time thinking this than you're probably not spending your time actually administering this to others.

Yet why are we so intolerant towards each other? As humans are we destined to be intolerant for ever? As mentioned earlier; on the spectrum of tolerance it is much more beneficial for all of us to understand our own intentions, to questions our own beliefs and to choose our own destinies. Only then can we make any distinction between what is useful intolerance and what is completely dangerous intolerance. It would be most useful to be intolerant to a culture that was determined to perpetuate murder and mayhem. There is a time for zero tolerance and I believe that time would be a time of life and death. If my life was at risk of harm or death from another human or beast, I would not tolerate another breath leaving my attacker. If anybody was at risk around me I would be as vigilant. This is an example of useful intolerance. Other than this it is simply a case of controlling your own vessel and keeping it safe from cosmic storms and meteor showers. We can find solace in the understanding that this comes naturally to absolutely no one. As with anything that is intended to be in good working order for as long as we can we must take time to maintain, clean and not overuse to the point that stress ensues to breaking point. There are items in our home that we take great care and maintenance of better than we do our own hearts and minds. We will need the resilience and accountability we spoke of earlier and we will need it in abundance because this kind of control does not come easily.

So you see that the question of what we tolerate or not is completely missing the point. The actual question is: what is our motivation and intentions in this life and are we doing everything that we can, every single day to ascertain congruence to our intentions by staying in close relation to our motivations? Are we providing appropriate stimuli to the ends of supporting this and if not; why not? If we can do this, what we tolerate or not, what we pay attention to and what – by proxy – we allow into our lives will adjust naturally and accordingly. It takes damn hard work and, although it is possible for all to achieve, it is anything but probable that most will. The easy road is far too wide and safe to be missed. The hard road is long and narrow and comes with much burden but where it leads is worth it. This is my personal understanding of the term: *"only the strong survive"* for it is only ourselves that we must ever be answerable to. As put by the great Frederick Douglass: *"I prefer to be true to myself even at the hazard of incurring the ridicule of others rather than to incur my own abhorrence."*

Designing Our Li(v)es

IN HIS CLASSIC TALE OF dystopia: "1984", George Orwell made famous the quote: *"He who controls the past controls the future..."* I chose to take an interest in this quote due to the context within the story in which the main character (Winston Smith) described a past occurrence that he remembered quite clearly which was documented by the governmental powers somewhat differently. He said that, although he had remembered the past in a certain manner, and was quite satisfied in its definiteness, this past only existed within his own mind as the government had orchestrated it from all other existence and that (when he would finally die) that memory would die along with him as would the truth that he perceived that he was sure had actually occurred. He was trapped in a society where the powers forged a history of their own making that suited their own agenda regardless of the perceived truth by any other individual. They would *create* a past that laid down the foundations for a future that suited their own intentions. Thus; *"He who controls the past controls the future..."*

The Illusory Memory Factor

OF OUR INTELLECTUAL FACTORS, MEMORY is a most interesting one and it is the only place where the past exists as it can never exist in the present moment except for in our minds. It would be paradoxical for it to be otherwise. Books, newspapers and video may document the past but serves only the intent to *remind* us of what has now past, of how things used to be and valuable lessons for the future. It stands as common sense that, if we have not read the book or seen the video than that particular piece of the past is unknown to us. Our past circumstance seems to hold the ability to dictate to us our present moment and the coming future in quite a hefty manner, yet if we had a past that was disturbed, violent or unproductive to our future, this would be the perfect circumstance to just let go. However this is exactly the past circumstances that have the greatest hold over us. Indeed the more intense the past the more fervently do we drag it into the present. However, even dragging a happy and privileged past into the present doesn't do us any good as it is in the aspect of the *attachment* to our past that can adhere us to memories that hinder us from impacting a productive forward trajectory in our lives. Attachments to the past, pleasant or otherwise, is counter-productive to being clear and free in the present moment which can allow us to be open to new and exciting experiences. The word "nostalgia", literally translates from its Greek roots as: *"going home to pain"*. A thought that is spent going back to times once gone, with a smile upon the face and a sadness in the heart. Yet, as powerful as it is, memory is *complete* creation. Of course, these things *may* have occurred in one way or another, yet for us to bring it to the present moment would mean to recreate what we *think* happened by utilising the intellectual power of memory. A recall has to take place. Pieces need to be filled in and a certain re-living must occur. Our *experience* is based solely on our *perception* and the programming that created that perception. Our recall of an experience no longer existing, *has* to be created thus is sorely adjusted as it is reformed as memory. Consider the courts. They call for numerous eye-witness accounts. They analyse where the stories collected conflict and where they match and fill the holes accordingly to fabricate as accurate an idea of the "truth" as possible based on the evidence submitted. That story then becomes recorded as actuality and the past is created. That past is used to choose and format the future. The actual actuality is that nothing exists from the past anymore but for the need of accountability *from* the past. Questions need answering people need blaming and punishing and we need reasons for doing the things we do and so forth. What then are we if we are not subject to our past? And what does this mean for those of us for whom it is the only thing we have that provides us with very strong implications of who we are, where we are from and where we are headed?

Depression and Futility

DEPRESSION IS SOMETHING THAT REGARDS its focus and attachments to be the regrets and injustices of the past and the seeming futility of the present moment with regards to creating a future that can be any better. Indeed a futility to even think of the future which eventually leads to anxiety: the *creation* of a futile and fearful future. The inability to see a purpose to life is a most deep and mired suffering. Depression is a sophisticated poison that works on every aspect of demotivation from life. The past, present and the future are left with a confusing lack of purpose. The stimulants, mental and physical, to facilitate depressions free-flow through the life and mind are expertly crafted and unforgivingly administered to its host.

> *"... and he who controls the present controls the future."*
>
> George Orwell-1984

With the understanding that the memory *is* creation, that the past is considered as our foundation which is *imperative* to the identity that forges our future trajectory, would it be deceitful of us to consider creating a past that worked better for us, thus tricking Cornelius into providing the base foundation needed for success? Would it be less deceitful to deny yourself the right to an opportunity to live free from the confines of pain linked to a tragic and abhorrent past?

But would this mean that we would be lying to ourselves and what would this do to the quality of our integrity? Considering what we have been discussing throughout this entire book, you will understand that we are all miraculous beings. Every one of us. Yet this unfortunately does not alter the idea that; if we were to hold our wishes in one hand and an absolute mess in the other, most would hesitate in choosing the wish whilst we would happily be blinded by the mess we have just unflinchingly slapped into our own eyes. You would also understand that, as mentioned prior, our memories are a matter of our own creation thus; we are always, in a manner of speaking, lying to ourselves at all times. So what makes us continue to feed ourselves with memories that do nothing to help us in building a positive foundation for success in life and beyond? Why do we choose to dwell upon thoughts that create a foundation of a destructive manifestation rather than a cultivation of pure energising bliss?

After one of my seminars, a young lady approached me who was experiencing a conflict of interest. She just had received a prestigious job offer from abroad yet she was considering turning it down as her father, who had just been invited back into the home that he was thrown out of months earlier, had begun beating on her mother. She said that she feared leaving her mother alone with her father due to what may happen to her. I venture to a short digression to mention that, as standard, I believe in simply exposing clients to the tools that they already have in their possession but are, for the reason of past programming, failing to utilise. I will guide instead of advise. Accountability is the key and the journey to accountability is empowerment. The responsibility is always within the hands of the beholder. The young lady was ready to throw opportunity to the dogs in order to suffer along with her mother. A gallant move many would believe yet I submitted to her the possibility that this choice could be quite a foolish and senseless one. I asked her first if she was aware of what her goal was, to which she replied that she did. I then asked her if she needed parental permission to pursue her goal. "Would you need a signature from your mother or father in order to chase your dream?" The lady again answered in the same fashion as the other times with a sound "no.", "Ok, so do you need their thumbs-up?" Again she answered "no". I then reminded her that her mother and father had forged their personal connection and relationship long before she was an aspect of their lives. A connection which continued when she was a child and which they perpetuated up to the present moment and that, as much as she may love her mother, she is making her own choices and that she is *choosing* what comes in and out of her life. Her miseries and her problems were something that she was refusing to let go of. I reminded her that if she was to fail in her goals it would be down to her own inability to make the choices that could bring benefit to her life. She left them to their story and she is happily now writing her own. She recently told me that it was the best move she made to distance herself from their entanglement and all it took was a step away from the unwanted obligations that she never asked for in the first place.

The Whisperings of Angels

Time to Rise

WE CAN SPEND OUR LIVES wondering why the people we love and care about made the most unwise decisions that have the most unbeneficial impacts on their lives. We can even spend our entire lives trying to convince them to repent of their ways and do otherwise, for their own good. However I believe that experience administers the greatest lessons and living our lives to the pinnacle of our abilities through all of the strives and trials is the best example we can hope to set for those whose lives we would care to impact. Doing otherwise is akin to lemmings following each other off of a cliff into a certain and utterly pointless doom.

Our choices were made for us as small children yet we can no longer claim the same regardless of how trying and impossible we believe our situation to be. We had little choice when we were tiny beings yet all the power necessary to change and define our existence is here right now and infinitely available to us all at all times. It doesn't matter if you've lost all of your money, if your dog has died or your wife left with the children, all of which are truly terrible things. Nevertheless it is always possible to prosper in every situation regardless of past traumas. With the examples of Victor Frankl, Louise Hay and Frederick Douglass to name only a few, who suffered traumas that would cause many to crumble and fade yet they became powerhouses of usefulness that will transcend decades and possibly even centuries to come. And more like them, born to atrocities every day, will rise to power and prominence to light a fire to the torch of human brilliance and potential. Like a game, progress is merely a process of discovery where the correct means to do something cannot be done through the denial of responsibility within the moment, the blaming of past occurrences or the failing to act as your greatest self in every single moment. Through the good and the bad, we all have had flimsy moments in our lives and will continue to do so however it is never an excuse for victimhood. My studies have been largely based, as is highly recommended, in the strength and resilience of the great men and women throughout all history who had a real reason to deny life due to the incredible levels of suffering they incurred yet the reason they continue to inspire to this day is due to their complete lack of victimhood and admirable drive for life. I have little time for sufferers and excuse makers. As mentioned throughout: accountability is the key.

Life is our very own personal journey and this, along with every journey in the cosmos has its pace set. There is no inertia! Stand still atop a great mountain and see the stillness, calm the breath, still the mind – there is no such thing. It is an illusion that aids us in creating a life that is pleasing to us. In the stillness the cosmos is electric with motion. Beneath the surface of the placid waters lays a fullness of movement and an abundance of life existing and writhing in ways that we can only wonder. In the stillness, within the casing of our bodies, a myriad of activities occur in every moment without pause. As we lay still in death that myriad continues to occur, returning us to the earthly state where we began. There is no stillness but in the perception we create, thus there is no chaos, there is no pain and there is no suffering but that which we create for ourselves or have yet to create a means away from. One of my greatest heroes: Louise Hay reminded me with great consistence, through a voice in my inner-ear, that all we ever suffer are our very own thoughts. We *may* have been caught up in a terrible past yet we alone are responsible for dragging it with us into the present moment. We may have to deal with things that we would rather not yet it is our own choice if we do so in misery. We have the choice in every passing moment to choose our thoughts and our responses. To create! And so create. And lie. Lie until you believe it.

Lies are Creation

BEST-SELLING AUTHOR NEIL GAIMAN, in his wonderful speech: *"Make Good Art"*, confessed to lying about his credentials in order to obtain a job that he knew he could be great at and the great Booker T. Washington who, in his determination to go to school, yet was having trouble being released from his job in the salt works on time to get there, set the clock forward half-an-hour in order to fool his boss into letting him go early which affected everybody who worked in the mines and could have got him into serious and painful trouble were he found out. Both men showcased the levels of their desire to succeed and both men felt guilty of their actions. Yet they were not lacking in integrity, they were compelled by their desire to succeed in their intentions. They had a resolve that they decided that nothing would stand between them and those intentions. Neil Gaiman was in turn determined to work for every magazine that he'd lied about in order to sate his guilt and Booker T. Washington felt an extraordinary flood of shame for a long time thus displaying the conflicts that men and women face when gratifying their desired goals and aims. It takes careful, specific intention and purpose to do what must be done and it takes a knowledge before-hand that not everything that must be done will be done comfortably. Read inspiring books daily. Create a library of intentions that will aid to strengthen you whenever doubt sets in. Arm yourself for the beautiful battle that is life yet do not forget that all of this is pointless without action. With the fuel of intention, the artillery of preparation and the appropriate *execution* you will find that you will either reach your destination or die trying, which is a far greater fate than those who die in insignificance and regret. The greatest battle being their entrance into this world and their greatest contribution to this earth being to the soil of which they become part of. Death is but a passing on of energy; the changing of the guard that comes to us all. Perpetuate your destiny beyond your own personal gain and know that, in the end, you simply *must* harvest that which you have sown. Be kind and be loving and loving kindness, in spite of the chaos that may ensue along the way, *will* be your just reward. Spearhead forward with selfish dreams of suppression and grandeur as you wish, yet be prepared for the fallout of your desires. The road of hate and misery is a cathartic one and creating fear in others may satisfy your self-induced suffering for the time-being, yet soon and ultimately, the famished footfalls of your reward will come to you, through you and leave its grim tread all over you.

... Rising to his feet, Kaden, although now imbued with a new confidence, knew it was but a drippling within the ocean of discontent he felt within his belly. He moved with caution toward the noise. Cold, metallic lemmings of perspiration raced down his forehead as he edged, creeping with tiny steps toward to front-door, hand outstretched in preparation for the handle. For each step closer he approached, the beast within his heart threatened to beat itself loose from his chest. His eyes fixated for shadows beneath the door and nothing was seen. A sweat-soaked grip twisted around the brass handle as well as within his aching throat and, with a slowness that lacked conviction, turned it to open the door. There, outside was nothing but the darkness that was the night. The cool night-breeze rushed across Kaden's face and he breathed hard once, emptying his lungs of the anxiety that constricted him. He felt foolish for the fear he had so openly exposed to himself and he laughed. "You *fool* Kaden." He whispered to himself as he closed the door and, as he turned back to face the warm and inviting lounge, he froze in fear at the sight of the human form of terror standing before him. Its shattered frame exposed the splintered, blood-stained bone and hanging, ragged flesh decorated in congealment and viscera which revealed the story of pain, suffering and betrayal. Through a wind-pipe flooded with clotted claret, it gargled its gruesome message. Dropping words in kind with broken teeth; "Kaden! - Your plan! - It worked! - I am with you forever my friend!" with a lolling, black tongue it repeated: "It has worked!" Kaden looked and saw hack marks on a wrist without a hand on the intruder, marks made by his own hand-axe... "Titus?!" Titus drew closer to Kaden, who had backed as far as he could to the door. Breath, riddled with a noxious pungency, heaved forth from drawn back lips and a face that was frozen in contortion and pain closed in on its unwilling host trapping him from moving. Kaden's own fear did the rest. "Kaden we are immortal! Your plan has worked!" Stated the cadaver "We are forever!"

As beings gifted with all the faculties of intelligence we will always, as a race, make decisions that are unhelpful or harmful – selfish and greedy. These may seem to reap great benefits to some to begin with (if you can bear to stand or realise the pain caused to others in their pursuit) and it can seem that there is nay a negative repercussion in sight. Yet for every action we perform and every word we say we weave the data into our being and it becomes part of us, recognised in the future and easier to perform without much thought. This consequently ripples outward into the world and creates a blueprint of who we have chosen to be. As this is being adopted by our system, the beings around us unknowingly receive the data of our character and begin to learn specific ways in how to deal with us. If this character is unintentional we will bear unintended fruit and we may not find the taste appealing. We may think that the prize is the all-important factor of the journey ahead but indeed our conduct throughout will write a story that will outlive our precious corporeal form. We will experience consequences that we have inadvertently requested through our actions and a fate that is thus deserving to our character. We can learn how to choose wisely and intentionally. The legacy that will tell the story of the choices we have made, will eventually and ultimately become our inescapable fate.

Responses and Reactions

THE REGARDED SOUND ADVICE SEEMS to be that the wise should strive, not to react unconsciously but to respond consciously. To take the time to think of an appropriate answer. To contemplate and conduct in a manner that we can be happy with. As mentioned, this is to attempt to take the time to respond in the stead of the impulsive reactions currently in charge of the reflex already in place. But what is that reflex and how did it get there in the first instance? We have some idea of how Cornelius was created and in great respect this is exactly how our current reflex actions were weaved in, unconscious repetition over the majority of our lives and, housed within our Cornelius, became the reflex actions that would occur without any conscious thought when stimulated by anything external. When I stared at that chopped down stump of the tree outside of my window, with the tiny sprig of life pushing through tenaciously, I knew that I had to - more so then just to be more aware of my conscious responses each day – truly understand exactly what it was that I wanted to convey for myself each day, consciously choosing my responses with the intent that they would replace the old and unwanted reactions that were programmed into me before I had any idea of what I wanted from this life (Lest we forget the spikey being that I had unconsciously practiced the responses for throughout my life that attracted nothing but trouble). I had to design the "me" that I wanted to be and I had to begin from the core outwards.

The Skill of Quick Decisions

OUR REACTIONS AND RESPONSES ARE stimuli to our minds and overall perspective and I regarded this as an incredibly empowering mission to take charge of. If I could somehow change the way I responded to the world – perhaps the world would respond in accordance to that change? I attempted to train myself to respond as my greatest self within most of the situations that I could think of. Of what to say when the nay-sayers, the scoffers and those dear to me began to feel threatened by, or simply didn't understand, what I was trying to achieve. Of being more intentional in my life and as many of the decisions therein. It made sense to me - as I began to relate more to my goals and the struggles I was encountering - to be adequately prepared for them, however, although I really loved this idea, I rarely had the gumption to see my convictions through. It took great care and continuous intention to try and respond as the best version of me on a regular basis as this was not something I was at all accustomed to doing. The spectrum of my ability was undisciplined and waned from day to day. Thus I began to feel anxious about my training and what I was doing to myself. I would ask if everybody went through the same thing and my thoughts spiralled into a cacophony of babble.

"If you are going to outwit the devil it's terribly important that you don't give him any advance notice."

Alan Watts

The change began to take form when I stopped training and just began being. I took it with ease in the stead of effort and, as I did so, my mechanics began to alter *simply*. I let go of the cavalcade of information data that I had accumulated and tried as often as I could, to focus on the miracle of the moment. I not only changed from the inside, it also changed my countenance on the out. My entire posture became strong as it had never been. I became more open as to what was happening around me and came to realise that there was *always* something to be thankful for. I began to listen more attentively, to both the voice of the world and to people when they spoke to me. Up till this point conversation was all about squeezing my word in when there was a gap in speech, therefore, I rarely heard what anyone was actually saying, I was just listening for the gaps so I could get my point across. I rarely remembered anybody's name, as it was of no interest to me and their point was just noise. When I began to listen, to become interested in what people were saying, something profound occurred. I heard their point of view and began to actually be interested in them. The more interested I was the more interesting I seemed to become. I realised that conversation, like anything, is a skill that, if respected, could bring a multiplex of benefits. One such benefit was in aiding me to filter out those who moaned and whinnied all the time as, when actually listening to this, it became unbearable and apparent as a waste of time. I had done my long term of whining about our precious planet and that was no longer something that I was interested in. As such, I sifted out the energy vampires and, as they faded with the sun of each new day, through relaxed, conscious conversation I met beautiful and amazing people and we enriched one another.

Over time this not only changed from my practiced and conscious choice of response they took place as my immediate and unconscious reactions. My responses to certain questions disappeared and reactions took their place, not exact words but the posture and mood and intention. The reaction to open the ear and the mind and relax the body now seemed default. Positive reactions where negative ones were once happily settled. Positive in the manner that my life's energy was replenishing and nourishing me instead of eating me alive. People began to recognise that I was a happy and actionable guy and my behaviour became infectious. Those around me would begin to speak more thoughtfully and I was told by many that I *felt* good to be around!

Growing up around martial arts I noticed the same thing happening in the dojo. When the students would drill techniques it begin with conscious movements, thinking and over-thinking, cumbersome and ineffective. Slow and unorthodox. The drilling was over-thought and under-done. The more thought went into the technique the more bumbling the techniques appeared. Yet once drilled over and over and over again, the thoughts became lost in the moment, the movements became smoothed and sheened where they we once rough and pinched. New ways became ingrained within the muscle and bone. Within the subconscious weaving was "the way that must be moved" in a crisis situation - programmed so that conscious thought was not necessary when action was needed. This may look to the outsider as very quick decision-making, however it is much more than that. It is the result of consistent action toward an intended purpose with ease. That is the purpose of the drill. To eliminate conscious thought, hesitation and the precious and vital time that can be utilised more effectively whilst the programmed reflex takes over.

> "*I don't know the knack of victory at all times, I have only learned how not to miss the right moment.*"
>
> Kenshin Uesugi

If our reactions are automatic responses, if we would want to make better decisions, we would do well to knowingly choose the responses we wish to convey, *who* it is we wish to convey at any given time, and become at ease with our intentions, so that we can begin to feel our thoughts, words and actions harmonised. *Designed by ourselves,* so that we no longer respond consciously when a snap decision is needed, instead we may *react* naturally and with purpose.

"The best antidote against anger is to be prepared, to have worked on the topic before something happens. It is good to be already wearing the parachute before jumping out of the window."

Lama Ole Nydahl

When we drill our responses, when our intentions have permeated our being, then we begin to *feel* the difference that takes place in our lives and we can realise that, even once we have created our vision for the future that we are emotionally invested in and the ability to snap to action when action is needed, that all this is *still* not enough and that's what *discipline* is all about.

Benjamin Fairbairn

Discipline within the Moment

UNDERSTANDING OUR GOALS, HAVING A vision for the future and being *emotionally invested* in the pursuit of those goals is all very good yet for those of us who are serious about gaining and maintaining the master-skill which takes us to a higher level will find that is just not good enough. On our journey things will always occur that will simply be out of our control, at a frequency that will be less than comfortable and which can threaten to hinder us at best and completely derail us at the very worst of times. We may very well love what we do and we may enjoy our pursuit to the utmost yet there will always be things that can cause us to become distracted and consistently create tiny injections of potent poisons that disintegrate our resolve and our determination causing us to starve our intentions of their precious sustenance. I could be talking about the song on the radio or the flashing of our phone, I could also be speaking of something more that requires our true attention like someone important exiting our lives or someone exciting coming into our lives. This may be our day to day job. Extreme pain and extreme joy can temporarily pull you off course from your life's goals and that is why we must learn to generate the ability to *re-attach* to the goal no matter what and that takes discipline!

> "It is only those who are persistent, and willing to study things deeply, who achieve the Master Work."
>
> The Englishman – Paulo Coelho's "The Alchemist"

202

I've heard the word discipline described as *"the ability to give ones-self a command and to follow it through to completion"*. I don't think it can be put better besides the inclusion of doing so in the face of great resistance, both internal and external and only those born of inhuman resolve can achieve this without putting certain specific measures in place.

To avoid misinterpretations, I daren't suggest meeting somebody with whom you would really like to spend time with is to be considered as an unnecessary distraction nor would I suggest the same for the passing of a loved one or the comforting of a friend in need. A partner leaving can be placed in that same bracket as it can cause intense suffering and grief. Leaving with the children can inflict a true drama onto life that can throw our world into flux and with the passing of a dear friend or loved one, care and time must be dedicated to maintaining or regaining a positive path. Engaging and fraternising in friendly company is neither to be considered as a distraction. This would be shutting yourself off from humanity and human relations, without which we would completely miss the entire point of being alive. Of what use are your goals and dreams, your great achievements or a great song if they solely amount to a smile in the dark?

In order to engage in any meaningful pursuit we must maintain our contact with the outside world, our compassion and our empathy.

My point is this: if you say you have a goal and are serious about attaining it then you will do well to make sure you are honest with yourself as to whether you really want it or not as this will mean having to sacrifice things that you don't want to in order to dedicate time to attaining those goals. The fact is that we will sometimes veer from the path due not to these things but to our lack of ownership and devotion to our own intentions, if that is not the case than your goal is incredibly unchallenging and you will need little aid in its pursuit. Creating the personality needed in order to attain your "goal", "desire", "dream" or "destiny" will take sacrifice and without strong intentions and measures to keep yourself in line you *will* become dis-engaged.

This dis-engagement comes in the nuances. As it is said: "*the devil is in the details*", and a lack of emotional engagement to our goals that brings derailment simply and frequently reveals the possibility that perhaps you never actually wanted to succeed here in the first place? Or it could be a sign that your life is changing for the better and that you must allow changes within yourself in order to meet with your intention.

What we must be aware of is the refraction of emotional engagement that can turn your destiny into a hobby. This is when, despite our strong emotional connection to our purpose, something equally close to us refracts and syphons our emotional artillery as we become convinced that this new thing is far more important. This is a true danger to the purpose and incredibly hard to recognise and, much like needing a gun and not having one, is best met with preparation. Buy the gun. Learn how to use it, when to use it, and then hope that you never have to. When we become aware of the disengagement that occurs we can begin to generate the ability to reattach to the purpose!

In times of extreme strife it can be difficult and seem impossible to even think of our dreams. This could mean that your current circumstance would need immediate and definite attention and must be sought at once as a matter of great importance as we must keep our minds and bodies sound to counter-act any disintegration with dedication. It is important to never lose the purpose to life and that is what reattaching to our goals, something that we have a high emotional investment in for the greater-good outside of our own needs, achieves.

We must know that these times are ahead and we must be prepared for them and not let them to the fickle whims of fate. Veering off of the path is as imminent as it is necessary. As Dr. Maxwell Maltz explained, in his ground-breaking study: Psycho-Cybernetics, we all have, whether we choose to recognise so or not, a cybernetic goal striving mechanism programmed deep within Cornelius, a destiny, which is strived towards sub-consciously, as subconsciously as the blinking of our eye and the beating of our heart, and on this journey we experience deviations from our course. This could be anything that diverts us from the pre-set destination within our Cornelius. Once the deviation is recognised it is corrected by the cybernetic system within the subconscious-mind and we are veered back onto track. Our intrinsic cybernetic system will always draw us back on track through the process of attending to the feedback we receive that tells Cornelius that we are veering and is adjusted accordingly. If your innate goal is to self-destruct, without awareness of that fact, and without the will to change, no amount of help will permanently veer you from this path to a new one and you will eventually destroy yourself in one way or another. The same thing happens when we consciously choose a goal that is not part of our original programming. We *will*, without any doubt, the moment that the struggle becomes something that we are not comfortable with and when we are forced to do things we dislike in order to achieve our set goals, veer from it and return to what we recognise as comfort. Then it will be up to *us* to reclaim our agenda, accept the negative feedback information, deal with it appropriately and accordingly with courage, *regain* control of our chosen course and strive on with diligence.

Noting the negative feedback for any future occurrences of the same. Only through changing the programming within our Cornelius can we ever hope to change the pre-set destiny within our intrinsic cybernetic system. It all comes down to re-configuring the way we think and perceive things in everyday life if they are not in harmony with what we want to achieve.

"Suppose you throw a coin enough times, suppose one day... it lands on its edge."

Kain – The Legacy of Kain

Emotional Quicksand

JOYOUS OR NAY, WHEN SOMETHING close to depression or some other emotional quicksand appears beneath us, what we enjoy to pursue becomes of very little importance. Sufferings such as anguish, anxiety and depression must not be ignored and neither should the professional advice and guidance on the matter. The responsibility however, is as ever, not that of the professionals. That responsibility is ultimately, and ever will be, our own.

"When a man finds that it is his destiny to suffer, he will have to accept suffering as his task."

Victor E. Frankl

Beyond medication, my personal saviour from depression was a real drive to understand and to remove myself from the catharsis of misery and from the inward focus of depression which, when put into one sentence can sound quite simple. Considering that I suffered from depression for over ten years without even realising it. Over time, however, I created counter-measures which were obviously no simple task to bide by as depression is a quicksand that begins its levels at the jaw, rapidly filling your maw and sucking your life away through a debilitating asphyxiation of our hope and perception. I found my way away from its consummation by realising its vital illusion. It is a disease that blinds you with your own suffering and blocks the light that leads to freedom. But the light is always there whether seen or not. I would venture that depression of today, although very real, is curried by an incredibly disorientated society. The depression that held me was also very real and lasted for a very real time. As always, the light lay in study of others and the more I learned about them the more I seemed to learn about myself and the nature of mankind. I read the personal accounts of men and women who had every reason to become engulfed by the smouldering black smoke of depression yet their stories told accounts of strength in the face of real and damning odds. Their bravery and their resilience served as guidance toward the light of freedom. World war two concentration camp survivor; Victor E. Frankl, once freed from his abysmal and torturous confines, perpetuated a form of therapy that he had developed before entering the hellish ordeal that focused on regaining the meaning and purpose in life: Logotherapy. Although he suffered extreme mental, emotional and physical torture of the highest degree and prolonged over a period of three years he stated in his book: "Man's Search for Meaning" that: *"We who live in concentration camps can remember the men who walked through the huts comforting the others, giving away their last piece of bread.*

"They may have been few in number but they offer sufficient proof that: everything can be taken from a man but one thing. The last of human freedoms: to choose ones attitude in any given set of circumstances. To choose one's own way."

Frankl heralded endurance. He suffered real pain and misery and no one would blame him if he were to choose to live his life with hatred, anger and resentment. Yet he chose love: *"The salvation of man is through Love and in Love."*

The Culture of Death as Doom

I HAVE EXPLAINED OF HOW I had an overwhelming fear of losing my loved-ones. I combatted this by being aware of every moment whilst being with them. When my Nanny's passing approached I felt as though I was standing at the edge of a precipice, arms aloud as I waited for a heaving gust to pull me to oblivion. Years before my Father's passing I was overwhelmed with fear of what would happen to me emotionally when it did. I knew that our relationship had unfinished business and I was petrified at leaving this unsung. I was also afraid as I knew that my mentality was gripping onto the edge of that precipice by the skin of my toes and knew that the slightest breeze would push me into mental instability. At this time I asked myself why I was so afraid of my loved ones leaving this place and I decided, there and then, to study death as perceived by cultures other than what I had known. I found that many cultures viewed death as a great passing from one existence to another and it was celebrated instead of mourned. Perhaps it was mourned privately, as never again seeing our loved-ones is a sting that sticks, but glory replaced misery and celebrating the life blurred the potency of mourning the death and gave life an epic new vibrancy. Death has never taken on a less frightening and more intriguing form to me than as I understand it now. I would suggest studying this topic further in your own time if you have never done so as I found the culture of death as doom to be a great contributor to the levels of anxiety and depression our society experiences.

The galvanised journeyman understands that in the rough terrain on the road to your purpose disappointments and painful challenges will be natural occurrences and it is in the knowing and dedication to that purpose that reveals life's potential. It was a purpose to life that imbibed strength and resilience to the examples throughout history and it is in the dedication to our purpose that will give us ours. Our destination becomes clear when there is something beckoning us on the other side. Still, hidden within the stinging bramble lies the seeping emotional quicksand. Plot your journey wisely and ready yourself for engagement to all manner of beasts and traps. You are the only one in control of your destiny and distractions are your responsibility to prepare for. If the progress is your process then it is your responsibility to maintain that progress and to manage your process. Create a vision for the life that you want. Create a means to bring that vision to life, design yourself as the most powerful person you can imagine and take full accountability. Regardless of life's emotional quicksand, contend to see your dreams through to its absolute completion.

What We Learn

THERE IS MUCH THAT I hope that can been gathered from these pages of mulling and musings yet my greatest wish is that we have, together, gathered a new clarity and belief that we are awesome beings upon this planet. We are capable of the most miraculous endeavours. From the mother who raises her children to be aware of their innate beauty and vital importance to the man who nurtures and protects his family and demonstrates the possibilities and diversities this world has to offer. To we who have loved and lost yet strived on diligently for the ultimate betterment of all. To all of us who are formulating, every day, a kaleidoscopic cavalcade of colourful, powerful energies around them at all times through the good moments and the not so good. To all the warriors of life who refuse to break and who fight on when the fight is hard.

We have found that there are reasons for the miseries that befall our days yet there is also a means to end our sufferings by finding purpose within them. By looking deeply into them and the lessons they can bring we need not despair as we know that everything changes and that we can affect those changes to fit our designed purpose. We have looked at some of the most admirable examples of women and of men who suffered greatly and achieved might, internal power and immortality through a wisdom and an awareness that their suffering was not life punishing, testing or laughing at them but perspectives of circumstances that only they had the power to change. We have learned that we have two programmes for life, one being held by

Cornelius our subconscious monkey and the other within our conscious, thinking mind and, if these do not match, then suffering ensues. Thus we know we have to change one of the programmes in order for our intentions to be harmonious with each other and this can fill us all with vitality for life until the brim is lost to an overflowing that just keeps going.

There is no book, no counsellor or no guru who can do the ultimate work for you and that revelation is so powerful. That only we have the power to take action against the things we find uncongenial to our mission to live and love and to perpetuate such. To cultivate the ability to cultivate. To learn how to learn and to love loving with no barriers to bequeathing its intense power to yourselves and all others. It is with great desire that we learn, when we deplete ourselves for the ones we love, we teach them that we consider ourselves expendable and unimportant to the greater cause and that, when they love they too may consider themselves expendable and unimportant in return. This is a fallacy of logic and a misconception of love's gift. It is my hope that we learn to love ourselves with such fullness that we give to our loved ones an authentic abundance that they can learn to perpetuate a love that does not deplete, instead it sustains, feeds and grows, long after the body has passed.

Know that your dreams are possible and promised to you should you be wise to the laws of their attainment and to your intentions - if they involve the harm and disarray of others as this will inflict injury and misery upon your own journey, as I attempted to illustrate through the fable of Kaden.

It is with this great hope that, as you experience trials, you can gain knowledge. Whoever may leave you, that you will never leave yourself and that you will always love yourself. This is most important in learning how to keep loving people around you. That as we augment our thinking, our environment and lives augments with us as will our circle of friends and loved ones.

The pusillanimous weaklings that gather like a gaggle of ducks to quack nonsense and peck at our resolve will waddle into the distance at the silhouette of the oncoming force of powerful and positive partners upon the horizon. Our journey will be supported by strength until the very end.

I leave you with this challenge: eradicate blame from your life entirely. Do not engage in pathetic conversation that attempts to cast blame onto you or unto themselves. Instead, from this moment forth, embrace all of your actions without judgement and seek to learn from all occurrences. Always question your motivations and enjoy your place in this world. Affect it accordingly with your brilliance for the betterment of all mankind. Understand the challenges that life brings and do not despair for it is in the challenges that we overcome and galvanise our spirits. Prepare yourself for a life with challenge and embrace it as the warrior that you can be. Do not force others to abide with you, to follow your individual perspective. They are on their journey as much as we are on ours. Be an inspiration through your life that encourages others to walk with you because they want to be around you.

With love – open your heart and live.

If you enjoyed this book (or if you did not enjoy it) please visit amazon.co.uk and leave a review

Also feel free to visit www.runninghyperion.com for more information on team and individual courses, to peruse and leave a message or to subscribe and join the mailing list for special offers and information on upcoming events!

Thanks for all your support!

I am forever grateful.

Benjamin.

38702712R00130

Printed in Poland
by Amazon Fulfillment
Poland Sp. z o.o., Wrocław